**Canadian Population Trends and Public Policy
Through the 1980s**

The Institute for Research on Public Policy was incorporated in 1972 as an independent non-profit organization. Its objective is to engage in research and analysis designed to improve the basis for informed choice and decision by Canadians on questions of public policy. The Institute's principal income is derived from an endowment fund supported by the private sector and the federal, provincial, and territorial governments.

There are two criteria for the selection of research topics. Projects must fall within policy fields of general interest to Canada in which significant change can be foreseen during the next five to 25 years, or where present policies are proving to be inadequate. Thus the need for, and expected use of, research results must be manifest.

The Institute undertakes to maintain conditions of inquiry that are conducive to high standards of professionalism and a learning environment.

The Board of Directors is responsible for the administration of the affairs of the Institute. The Council of Trustees advises on the development of a research program, on the selection of, and designation of priority to, research topics, and on related matters of policy. The execution of the research plan and the administration of publication policies are responsibilities of the President.

Final decision on publication of a manuscript rests with the President. That judgement is informed by the advice of external assessors as to the quality of a manuscript and the contribution it should make to improving the basis for informed choice and decision.

Publications of the Institute are offered as searching inquiries into subjects worthy of public consideration and policy formation. The contents of publications are the responsibility of the authors; the Institute as such does not take a position thereon.

CANADIAN POPULATION TRENDS AND PUBLIC POLICY THROUGH THE 1980s
Leroy O. Stone and Claude Marceau

CANADIAN POPULATION TRENDS AND PUBLIC POLICY THROUGH THE 1980s

Leroy O. Stone and Claude Marceau

with the assistance of
Gail Grant Akian
Hélène Gaudry Seni
Ann Connolly McCoomb

.

.

Published for the
Institute for Research on Public Policy
by
McGill–Queen's University Press
Montreal and London

©Institute for Research on Public Policy 1977
Paper bound edition reprinted 1978

ISBN 0 7735 0287 4 (cloth)
ISBN 0 7735 0288 2 (paper)

Legal Deposit first Quarter 1977
Bibliothèque nationale du Québec

Printed in Canada by
Imprimerie Gagné Ltée

PREFACE

This report is a synthesis of opinions about problems that will confront Canada during the next 15 to 20 years. Public policy issues related to Canadian population trends are the major subject of the discussion that follows.

The report is addressed mainly to Canadians who are concerned about the future of their country and wish to have a concise introduction to a variety of important social and economic problems that are substantially connected to trends in the size, geographic distribution, and composition of Canada's population. Politicians, public officials in all spheres of Canadian government, and other citizens who wish to improve the scope of their identification of Canadian problems are the prime intended audience. Unfortunately, however, the report cannot be concise and also serve as an elementary textbook for those who have had no previous introduction to the field of population studies.

The following survey of Canadian population trends and related public policy issues is strictly introductory. Extended clarification of any particular population trend or public policy issue is deliberately avoided. The reader who wishes such clarification may find a helpful starting point in the bibliographic references. In effect, the aim of this brief review is to touch a number of significant bases in the field of public issues related to Canadian population trends. The reader should emerge from studying this report with a broader perspective from which to analyse or priorize specific public policy issues.

Some readers might think that a more valuable attempt at widening their perspective would result if the discussion were not so strongly concerned with population trends. The decision to so restrict the scope of this volume is a direct result of an implied instruction of the Executive Committee of the Institute for Research on Public Policy (IRPP). The general objective of this project was initially set forth in an IRPP brochure as follows:

> The first project . . . a study of population trends and developments and identification of problems . . . is expected to identify a wide range of public policy issues which may be examined as the scope of the Institute's research activities widens. . . . The object of this project is the identification of problem areas and their implications for Canadian public policy and for collective action in Canada, through a study of demographic trends and developments in Canada to the year 2000, with emphasis on the decade of the 1980's.

PREFACE

Starting in April 1975, three broad classes of activity were undertaken to develop this report: (1) collecting and extending (as necessary) some of the existing projections of selected Canadian demographic trends into the 1980s; (2) eliciting from literature and from experts commentaries in connection with the main concern of the project; and (3) critically synthesizing the information gathered into a final project report of which this volume is a summary. The literature studied included reports from conferences, commissions, and committees, as well as books and articles in a variety of fields. The experts who were consulted represented several disciplines and professional affiliations and were from across Canada (see appendix).

The main body of this volume consists of four chapters, followed by a short appendix, references, and a selected bibliography. The first chapter is introductory, and the second chapter comments on the pattern of selected plausible future Canadian demographic trends. This commentary helps to set the stage for a discussion of important public policy issues connected with Canadian population trends. The discussion of public policy issues is the subject of the third chapter. The issues are grouped under three very broad headings that highlight pertinent aspects of population trends: growth of the national population and labour force, geographic distribution of Canadians, and socio-economic composition of the populace. Chapter four reviews some of the available evidence on the scope of government concern in the field of population policy, where population trends are the direct objects of policy-making. A focus on population policy seemed worthwhile in view of the general theme of this project, of the paucity of literature on Canadian government activity in the field, and of the recent upsurge of federal government attention to population policy issues. This chapter was written by Claude Marceau, while the remainder of the text was drafted primarily by myself.

The appendix provides information concerning three major seminars that were organized in the conduct of this study. Experts from across Canada spent three days discussing public policy issues, research on Canadian population trends, and desirable emphasis in IRPP research.

It should be noted that this volume omits an entire chapter that was presented in the final project report. The chapter in question contained a list of 86 possible research areas which would contribute to well-informed public debate and policy formation on selected public policy issues. The list can be obtained by writing to IRPP.

A word of thanks is due to the large number of individuals who contributed significantly to the completion of this project, and the authors apologize to anyone whose name has inadvertently been omitted below. The main project team included C. Marceau, G. G. Akian, H. Gaudry Seni, A. C. McCoomb, and J. O. Simard. Substantial commentary was occasionally provided on request by R. Breton, A. W. R. Carrothers,

F. Denton, G. Doern, G. Hodge, N. Keyfitz, R. Lachapelle, R. McInnis, M. Pinard, J. Porter, A. Raynauld, and T. Ringereide. Useful contributions were made by all of the participants at the 15–19 September seminars, and these individuals are listed in the appendix. Important data series were made available by F. Denton, B. Spencer, and Z. Zsigmond. Significant occasional assistance was provided by F. Aubry, C. Desjardins, I. Ducharme, S. Fletcher, V. Hansen, H. Hayes, L. Morneau, F. Sabourin, and D. Trotzier.

Finally, the following persons were kind enough to review and provide comments on an earlier draft of this report: D. Bairstow, L. J. Byrne, L. Downey, J. Henripin, F. Kelly, N. Keyfitz, H. Laframboise, R. Lachapelle, L. Marsden, and I. Timonin. None of these individuals is responsible for any errors or omissions that may exist in this volume.

LEROY O. STONE

Contents

Charts

1

RELATING POPULATION TRENDS TO PUBLIC POLICY ISSUES

There is something unnatural about the attempt to identify public policy issues through the study of population trends.[1] Usually one is led to the identification of public policy issues through a concern about specific problems in the welfare[2] of the nation or of particular communities. Population trends may be a more or less important aspect of some of the identified issues.

Canadians have historically used the study of a variety of trends as a helpful vehicle in anticipating public policy issues. In so doing they have tended to emphasize the study of trends in aspects of the economy. Indeed, with the exception of such fields as military preparedness and public health, the concept of public welfare has historically been interpreted largely in terms of aspects of the production and distribution of income and wealth.

Since the early 1960s, Canadians have continued to become more concerned with public well-being. It is fashionable now to speak about aspects of the quality of Canadian life with which income and wealth are only rather indirectly (though often importantly) connected. Prominently related to many such aspects of life in Canada are the growth, composition, and distribution of the population. These concepts are clarified below. Today politicians are urging Canadians to think about the "kind of Canada we want" in terms of dimensions of Canadian communities that sometimes include population trends. It is, therefore, timely that the study of population trends be included among the avenues customarily used as aids in the anticipation of public policy issues.

1. The intended meanings of the phrases *public policy issue* and *population trends* are indicated in section 1.1.

2. The concept of *public welfare* (or *social welfare)* is often used to refer to the economic condition of, or income transfer programs for, a small segment of disadvantaged people in society. In this text public welfare pertains to a variety of aspects of the well-being of the entire society. A phrase that conveys much of the same broad meaning is *quality of life,* and the meaning goes far beyond the economic condition of the nation or income transfer programs. For example, nutrition and health, quality of housing, and opportunities to pursue useful social roles are also included, among other aspects of life, in the broad concept of public welfare used in this text.

1

1.1 Some Basic Concepts

It is advisable to comment briefly on the meaning that will be attributed to two concepts used in this text. The concepts in question are *population trends* and *public policy issues.*

The term *population trends* refers to the main patterns of change in regard to the size, geographic distribution, and composition of population, as well as to the underlying population processes of fertility, nuptiality, mortality, morbidity, mobility (geographic and social), learning, work, and recreation.[3] Changes in the size, distribution, and composition of population are the direct result of the operation of such processes.

It may be helpful to offer additional remarks about some of the concepts mentioned in the preceding paragraph. Trends in *population size* are most often identified by using data on the absolute number of people or on rates of change in that number.

Generally, the concept of *population distribution* refers to the manner in which a population is spread over a given territory. Various aspects of population spread can be measured. For example, a territory (such as Canada) may be subdivided into a number of regions (e.g. provinces) and the proportion of the territory's total population that lies in each region is measured. Indeed, the collection of such proportions is often intended when one refers to *the distribution of population with respect to the specified regions.* Other aspects of population distribution include the degree of concentration of population in specific settlements such as metropolitan areas (or among parts of such settlements), the pattern of dispersion of population about a given point (e.g. a major urban centre like Toronto), or a series of points (e.g. the border between Canada and the United States), the relative sizes of selected centres, or the density of population in certain areas. The allocation of Canada's population among provincial, urban, rural, and metropolitan areas is an aspect of its geographic distribution.

The concept of *composition of population* pertains to the manner in which the population is allocated among the categories of several demographic, social, and economic attributes. For example, the allocation of Canada's population among the categories of age (such as children, young adults, middle-aged adults, and the elderly) is known as its *age composition.* There are also many other kinds of compositions, such as mother tongue, marital status, educational attainment, and occupation.

Brief clarifying comments about some of the population processes

3. *Pattern of change* should be understood to include the case of no change. It should also be assumed that the process of identifying a specific pattern of change (trend) in a series of statistics involves some element of interpretation and judgement.

mentioned above are also in order. *Fertility* and *nuptiality* are the processes of bearing children and forming (or dissolving) families. *Mortality* and *morbidity* refer to death and illness, respectively. *Geographic mobility* is the process of changing location in space, particularly *residence change,* as well as commuting between the place of residence and the places of work and recreation. *Social mobility* involves changing certain of one's personal characteristics, such as occupation. (The reader who wishes to obtain a more extended introduction to the concepts just discussed, and particularly to population processes, should consult Bogue (1969), or another general textbook in substantive demography.)

An *issue of public policy* may be formulated as a question (including a network of closely related subsidiary questions) that government policy-makers, at any level of government, either are attempting to answer, planning to attempt to answer, or should reasonably be expected to attempt to answer.[4] The answer adopted is the *embraced policy,* and an issue may be said to exist either when a specific alternative answer has not been embraced or when a key "public" contends that the wrong answer has been embraced. It is not necessary to explicitly formulate an issue as a question, however, since the pertinent query can readily be inferred from a declarative statement pointing out a problem that policy-makers will or should attempt to resolve.

1.2 Some Qualifications

Population trends are one of the important sources of Canadian social problems.[5] For example, the increasing concentration of the national population in a handful of metropolitan areas is considered by many to

4.   Public policy-making can be defined to include activities of non-governmental organizations (labour unions, religious organizations, ethnic associations, etc.). This would have entailed writing a much longer volume within the six months available. It seemed advisable to concentrate on the actual and prospective policy-making of the constituted representatives of the people (elected politicians) and their delegates (public officials), whose field of operation is probably wider than that of any other kind of organization concerned with public policies in Canada.

5.   The usage of the concept *social problems* is much broader in this text than is generally the case with the mass media. Often, in the media a social problem is thought to be some undesirable state of affairs concerning a specific group within society or the relations among groups or individuals. The broader concept used in this text also covers states of affairs concerning the economy, the environment, and other matters that do not relate directly to the characteristics of, or relations among, groups and individuals. The concept, social problem, focuses on the existence and source of concern about a given state of affairs rather than on the specific content of the state of affairs.

be a significant source of problems, which in turn forms a basis for substantial issues of Canadian public policy. Population trends are also weighty factors that influence the importance or the solution of other problems. For example, the gravity of the problem of poverty in Canada depends partly on changes in the distribution of the population among certain key social groups. Issues of public policy tend to arise when significant groups of citizens wish to eliminate or alleviate the perceived social problems. Through the direct connection of population trends with some social problems, at least indirect relations may be identified between such trends and public policy issues.

However, several qualifications must be noted before attempting at least partly to identify Canadian public policy issues through a study of population trends. Firstly, in focusing upon those public policy issues that are substantially related to population trends, we must be careful to avoid giving the impression that these are the only major public policy issues. In fact, many important social problems exist for which population trends form a factor of only marginal significance.

Secondly, even when population trends are strongly related to particular public policy issues, they are often only part of the explanation or the solution of the problems that gave rise to the issues.

Thirdly, most references to policy issues in this report are stated at a general level. Concrete debate or policy development concerning such issues would probably require some effort to break down general statements into a series of subsidiary policy issues. For example, section 3.4.4 of chapter three mentions the preservation of a desirable balance between the relative weights of French- and English-speaking groups in the political life and the culture of Canada. Concrete policy developments concerning this issue would involve the framing of subsidiary issues, including such matters as the composition of immigration, family planning practices, and language of work.

1.3 Nature of the Relationship

With the foregoing qualifications in mind, it seems worthwhile to speculate briefly about how population trends may be linked with public policy issues. For the most part the linkage is indirect, through connections between population trends and certain social problems. This indirect relationship may occur in at least two ways.

Firstly, certain aspects of population trends are the direct objects of public debate and policy-making, because they are perceived to embody features that are intrinsic to the well-being of Canadian communities. For example, the linguistic balance in the population between French and English is viewed by many as such a feature, and a policy option concerning special efforts to encourage French-speaking immigrants to

Canada is currently being debated as a means of maintaining a desirable linguistic balance. (Linguistic balance is an aspect of the composition of population.)

Secondly, the incidence and the magnitude of certain social problems depend markedly upon population trends that are unlikely to be the direct objects of public policy. For example, the size of the elderly population of Canada during the next 25 to 50 years is unlikely to be a variable for which public policy will deliberately be formulated. However, this variable is crucially involved in the degree of pressure upon tax revenues arising from policies aimed at offering needed social services to Canada's older population.

There is significant overlap among the different kinds of connection between population trends and public policy issues. This point will be illustrated in chapter three, where more concrete comments about specific connections between population trends and public policy issues will be provided. In preparation for this discussion, a review of one set of plausible future population trends is in order.

2

FUTURE CANADIAN POPULATION TRENDS

2.1 Purpose and Content of the Projections

It is necessary to speculate about the years ahead in the process of attempting to signal future public policy issues. This speculation can put forward "data" about the future either to identify certain consequences if present trends are continued or to delineate possible policy targets and their requirements. For example, future changes in each province's share of Canada's total population can be projected on the basis of the assumed continuation of recent trends in the determinants of provincial population growth. The general pattern of these projected changes may be judged highly undesirable, and as a result policies aimed at changing the trends may be debated. In the course of such a debate additional projections may be used to indicate how alternative trends can be achieved.

This chapter comments on the demographic trends that are indicated by a collection of projections for the Canadian population. The collection has been extracted from the works of various authors writing since the mid-1960s. The projections deal with a variety of variables, and the numbers shown in the original publications have typically been altered somewhat to achieve improved internal consistency among the different data series. The coverage of variables includes growth; population composition with respect to sex, age, mother tongue, and schooling; provincial and rural-urban distribution; labour force size; labour force composition with respect to sex, age and marital status; numbers of households and families; and housing.

A number of factors have dictated the limited coverage of variables, the lack of detail given about each variable, and the decision to merely collect and adjust already existing projections rather than to develop new ones. Among these was the fact that only six weeks were available for the preparation of data. It would not have been possible in that time period either to cover a substantially greater variety of variables or to do fundamental projections research.

In designing this chapter it was decided that there would be a central set of projections of the population by sex and age to which all the other numbers would be "anchored" in a desirable way. (For example, if we have projections from two separate sources concerning population and

7

families, we should ensure that the pertinent totals bear a relationship that is reasonable in the light of historical experience and substantive knowledge in demography.) Partly because of the widespread use and the availability of the population projections published by Statistics Canada (Cat. No. 91-514, 1974), it seemed advisable to choose the central set of projections used in this volume from among the 16 alternative series prepared by Statistics Canada.

From among these 16 projections, Statistics Canada selected four "to indicate the range of future population of Canada and the provinces" (Cat. No. 91-514, 1974, p. 59). Some critics have expressed doubt that the 16 possibilities, and particularly the four that were chosen, provide the most suitable basis for sketching a range of plausible future values for the population growth in certain provinces (especially Quebec, Alberta, and Saskatchewan). However, the immediately available alternatives do not provide as wide a range for the possible total population of Canada as that provided in the Statistics Canada selection. Furthermore, most users of projections are already familiar with the Statistics Canada series. Accordingly it was decided that Series A and Series C, two of four key series chosen by Statistics Canada, would be highlighted in this volume. A summary of the assumptions underlying these series is as follows:

Summary of Fertility and Migration Assumptions[1] Underlying Projections A, C, Canada, 1972-2001

Title and fertility assumption	Assumed total fertility rate for Canada by 1985	Migration assumptions	
		International (net gain of population each year)	Interprovincial (gross movement of people each year)
Projection A: High fertility	2.60	100,000	450,000
Projection C: Low fertility	1.80	60,000	435,000

[1] The mortality assumption is the same for all projections.
SOURCE: Statistics Canada, Cat. No. 91-514, 1974.

The data concerning the future, provided below, are not predictions in the sense that they comprise positive assertions as to what is expected to happen. For example, the projection that in 1991 the population of Canada will lie somewhere between 26.6 and 30.2 million is in fact not a prediction. This range of figures merely indicates that a set of assumptions concerning the future ranges of values of national rates of mortality, fertility, and migration logically imply the above-mentioned range of 1991 population sizes. If the assumptions hold true in the future, then the actual 1991 population will lie somewhere within that range.

Instead of viewing the following figures as positive predictions of what will happen in the future of the Canadian population, the reader should see them as a systematic speculation about future values for the variables to which the figures pertain.

2.2 Size and Geographic Distribution

2.2.1 International perspective The group of highly developed countries, of which Canada is a member, contains a gradually shrinking percentage of the entire world population. The more developed countries contained about 30 percent of the world's population in 1970. This percentage has been projected to decline to a level somewhere between 22 percent and 28 percent by the year 1990 (U.N., 1966, p. 23). These countries are contained within Europe, U.S.S.R., North America, Japan, Temperate South America, Australia, and New Zealand.

For North America, which partly includes Canada and the United States, U.N. projections speculate in favour of continued population growth to the end of this century. However, the share of the world's population residing in this region is projected to decline slightly from an estimated 6.3 percent in 1970 to 5.7 percent in 1990 (U.N., 1966, pp. 134–36).

The Organisation for Economic Co-operation and Development (OECD) has published a series of projections for its member countries (OECD, 1974), and table 2.1 shows average annual growth rates derived from the OECD publication with respect to selected countries located mainly in northwestern Europe and North America. Canada and the United States show the highest *projected* growth rates from the mid-1960s to the mid-1980s, among the nine selected OECD members listed in table 2.1. Average annual rates substantially above one percent per annum are projected for these two countries, whereas rates significantly below one percent per annum are projected for the selected western European countries.

TABLE 2.1

Historical and Projected Rates of Population Growth,
Canada and Selected OECD Countries, 1965–70 to 1980–85

Average annual growth rates

Country	1965–70	1970–75	1975–80	1980–85
Belgium	0.5	0.3	0.1	0.1
Canada	1.9	1.6	1.8	n/a[1]
Finland	0.3	- 0.2	- 0.2	- 0.2
France	0.8	1.0	1.1	1.1
Ireland	0.6	0.7	0.9	1.0
Italy	0.7	0.6	0.5	0.5
Sweden	0.8	0.6	0.6	0.5
United Kingdom	0.5	0.5	0.5	0.5
United States	0.9	1.4	1.4	1.4

[1] Not available

SOURCE: OECD, 1974, Table I-4.

2.2.2 National and provincial growth   For the period from 1971 to 1991, recent Statistics Canada population projections show average annual growth rates generally between one and two percent. Chart 2.1 indicates that population growth rates have undergone a steady decline since 1951. Over the projection period 1971 to 1991, no return to the 2.5+ percent growth rates of the 1950s is envisaged. These declines in growth rate are largely the result of a substantial fall in birth rates which began in the closing years of the 1950s, and the Statistics Canada projections generally assume for the next 15 years levels of fertility that are substantially below those of the 15 years immediately following the Second World War.

The range of growth rates envisaged in the Statistics Canada Series A and Series C projections implies a total national population in 1991 of somewhere between 26.1 and 30.2 million. In other words, these series speculate on an additional population of somewhere between 5 million and 8.5 million between 1971 and 1991. The 1981 population is projected to lie between 24.0 and 25.2 million. Thus, these series project a minimum addition of three and one-half million Canadians between 1971 and 1981. The Statistics Canada estimate of the total population of Canada on 1 June 1975 indicates that an addition of 1.3 million people has already occurred since 1971.

Both in the cases of the provinces and the country as a whole, the

Chart 2.1

Historical and Projected Rate of Population Growth, Canada
1951–56 to 1986–91

CANADA

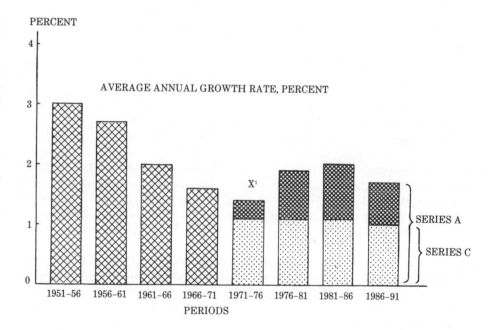

¹The symbols "X" on each chart indicate the first point in the projection data. Prior to that point the figures are historical estimates.

SOURCE: Statistics Canada, Cat. No. 91–514, 1974, pp. 101–51.

Statistics Canada projections speculate on no return in the near future to the relatively "heady" rates of growth of the 1950s and the early 1960s. Interprovincial differences in the rate of population growth are expected to persist through 1991, and, as a result of these differences, some provinces may lose in their share of the national population.

2.2.3 Urbanization and metropolitan growth   Canada will continue to participate in the world-wide phenomenon of growing urbanization. Compared to the 1950s and 1960s, the five-yearly increase in the level of urbanization (the proportion of the population residing in urban centres)[1] is projected to moderate over the next 15 years. Nevertheless, the Economic Council of Canada projects that about 85 percent of the 1991 population of the country will reside in urban centres, compared with 76 percent in 1971 (see chart 2.2). All of the five major regions of Canada are expected to show advancing urbanization during the next 15 years.

Although census metropolitan areas are not conterminous with the urban centres of 100,000 or more, some reflections on the projected growth of Canada's largest urban agglomerations were provided by the Ministry of State for Urban Affairs (MSUA) in a 1975 set of projections (see Canada, Ministry of State for Urban Affairs, 1975b).

According to these projections (after modifications aimed at improving their consistency with Series A and Series C), somewhere between 14.9 and 16.9 million people will reside in the twenty-two 1971 census metropolitan areas in 1991 (see chart 2.3). An increase of nearly one million is expected in the population of these metropolitan areas between 1971 and 1976. (According to Statistics Canada estimates, an increase of nearly nine-tenths of a million had already taken place between 1971 and 1974.) Another increase of at least two-thirds of a million is the speculation for the 1976 to 1981 period. Toronto and Montreal are each expected to reach beyond three million in size by 1991, compared to about two and three-quarter million each in 1971. Vancouver is projected to add at least one-half million residents to its 1971 population of 1.1 million. On the whole, however, the MSUA projections assume that metropolitan areas will participate in the general decline of national population growth.

2.3 Growth and Composition of the Labour Force

Labour force growth rates higher than those of the national population are projected to persist during the next 15 years. For example, whereas a

1. In this text, *urban area* means a densely settled, built-up area of at least 1,000 in population. For a related discussion, see Stone (1967), section 1.3.

Chart 2.2

Historical and Projected Percentage Urban, for the Population of Canada[1] and its Major Regions 1851 to 1991

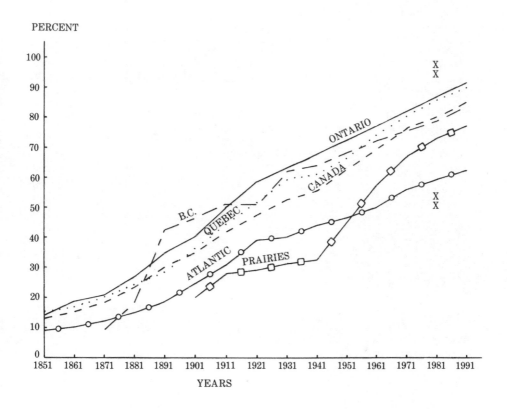

PERCENT

[1]Excluding Yukon and Northwest Territories.

SOURCES : Stone, 1967, Table 2.2. Statistics Canada, *1971 Census,* Cat. No. 92–709. Economic Council of Canada, 1967, Table 7.4.

Chart 2.3

**Historical and Projected Population for 1971
Census Metropolitan Areas, Canada
1951 to 1991**

Canada

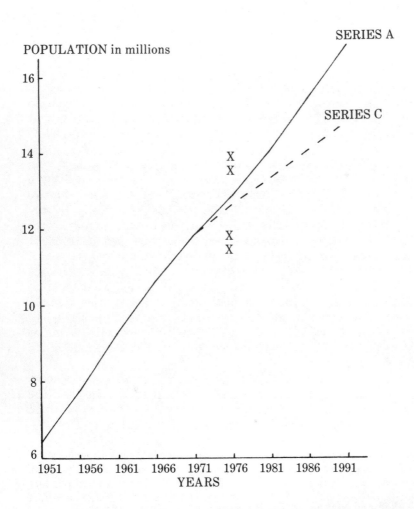

SOURCES: Statistics Canada, Cat. No. 91–514, 1974; *1971 Census,* Cat. No. 92–702, Table 2. Ministry of State for Urban Affairs, 1975b.

"minimum" population growth rate of 23 percent is envisaged for the 1971–1991 period, the "minimum" labour force growth rate envisaged is 52 percent. The corresponding "maxima" are 40 percent for the population and 59 percent for the labour force.[2]

Chart 2.4 shows the pertinent projected totals by sex and marital status. By 1991 the labour force is projected to reach somewhere between 13.1 and 13.7 million, compared with 8.6 million in 1971. As early as 1981 the labour force is projected as exceeding 11.5 million. Especially significant for the composition of the labour supply and for the changes it will portend within the family is the envisaged rise in the number of married women in the labour force. The absolute number of married women in the labour force is projected to more than double between 1971 and 1991, from 1.6 million to at least 3.3 million under the Series A and Series C projections. Even between 1971 and 1976 a rise of at least 25 percent is projected in the number of married females in the labour force; and between 1971 and 1981 this number is projected to jump by 60 percent or more.

Females as a group will continue to show substantially higher than average rates of labour force growth over the next 15 years, according to the Series A and Series C projections. However, the gap between the two labour force growth rates is projected to narrow substantially by the onset of the 1980s. Exceptionally high rates of female labour force growth have been observed since the 1950s. As recently as the 1966–71 period, the female labour force grew at an *average* annual rate of 5.4 percent. An even higher range of possible female labour force participation rates is projected for the 1971 to 1976 period, that is, from 5.8 to 6.0 percent on an average annual basis. (The Statistics Canada Labour Force Survey estimate for the 1973–74 period is 5.5 percent.) In sharp contrast the average annual rate of labour force growth for males was 2.3 percent in 1966–71 and is projected to lie within the range of 2.6 percent and 2.8 percent in 1971–76.

However, the average annual rate of labour force growth is projected to decline below the 1971–76 levels as early as 1976–81. By 1981–86 the projected average annual rate of labour force growth for both sexes is in the range of 1.7 to 1.9 percent, compared with 3.3 percent in 1966–71.

2.   The labour force projections presented below were prepared especially for this study by Professors Frank Denton and Byron Spencer on behalf of Canadian Economic Services. Mr. Denton was asked to employ a crude method to produce relatively aggregated projections within a short time. It was felt that this effort would be sufficient for him to forecast some major trends in the likely future labour force growth. Totals were based on the Statistics Canada Series A and Series C population projections. The figures pertain to annual averages of the mainly civilian non-institutional labour force. Excluded are members of the armed forces, Indians on reserves, inmates of institutions, and residents of the Yukon and Northwest Territories.

Chart 2.4

Historical and Projected Labour Force by Sex
Canada, 1961 to 1991

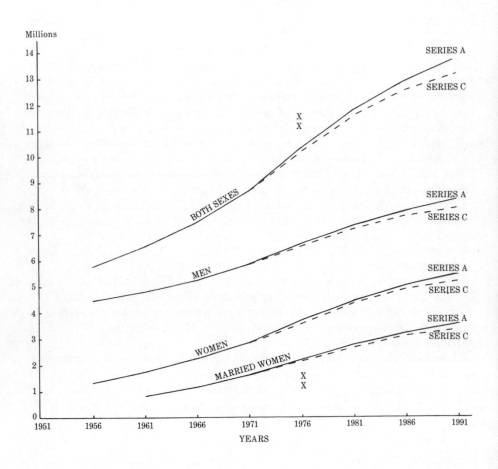

SOURCES: Unpublished projections prepared by Frank Denton of Canadian Economic Services. Statistics Canada, Cat. No. 91-514, 1974, pp. 101-51.

Even the average annual growth rate of the female labour force is projected to show a marked decline from 5.4 percent in 1966–71 to somewhere between 2.4 and 2.6 percent in 1981–86. By 1986–91 still lower labour force growth rates are envisaged.

Chart 2.5 provides the curves for three summary measures of the demographic composition of the labour force. The data in this chart are drawn from Series A numbers only, since the Series C numbers did not imply substantial differences with the curves shown on the chart. As the foregoing discussion implies, the percentage of the labour force that is female is expected to rise substantially, from 33 percent in 1971 to 40 percent in 1991. Among females in the labour force, the percentage married is envisaged to rise from 57 percent in 1971 to 64 percent in 1991.

2.4 Changes in Socio-Demographic Composition of Population

This section presents a collection of projections concerning the distribution of the Canadian population with respect to sex, age, mother tongue, educational attainment, and school enrolment. Historical data on the ethnic origin composition of the population are also provided.

2.4.1 Age distribution   As is well known, the post-war baby boom led to a substantial "rejuvenation" of the age structure of the Canadian population—the proportion of young children rose significantly. By 1971 there was a marked rise in the proportion of young adults in the population. However, with the rapid decline of the birth rate starting approximately at the end of the 1950s, the growth rate of the group of young children fell sharply, and their proportion in the age distribution has declined (from 12.3 percent in 1951 to 8.4 percent in 1971). In the meantime the proportion of older Canadians has increased steadily, though not dramatically.

The Statistics Canada Series A and C projections do not envisage a major shift in the trend for Canada's age distribution between 1971 and 1991 (see chart 2.6). The proportion of young children continues to be at a relatively low level compared to the 1950s. The "movement" of the post-war baby boom through the age structure is tracked adequately, showing gradual decline in the proportion of young adults and a tendency towards rise in the proportion of middle-aged adults.[3] By 1991 the baby boom survivors have not yet reached retirement age and above, thus they fail to impart any significant impetus to the growth rate of the older population. The proportion of older persons in the population merely continues its very gradual increase through 1991.

3.   Although the proportion of young adults may fall, their absolute number may continue to rise.

Chart 2.5

Selected Labour Force Statistics, Historical and Projected
Canada, 1956 to 1991

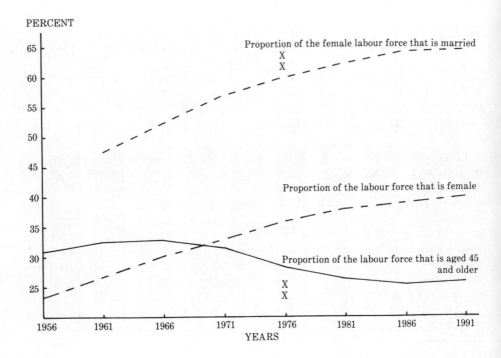

SOURCES: Unpublished projections prepared by Frank Denton of Canadian Economic Services. Statistics Canada, Cat. No. 91–514, 1974, pp. 101–51.

Chart 2.6

Historical and Projected Age Distribution
of the Population of Canada
1951 to 1991

(Series A)

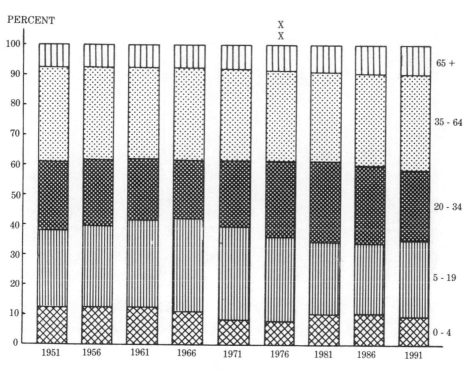

YEARS

Chart 2.6 cont'd

Historical and Projected Age Distribution
of the Population of Canada
1951 to 1991

(Series C)

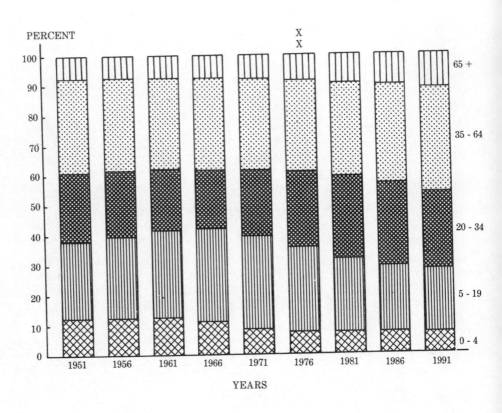

SOURCES: Statistics Canada, Cat. No. 91–514, 1974, pp. 91–150; *1971 Census,* Cat. No. 92–702, Table 2.

Although the older population does not show a spectacular advance in its percentage of the total population by 1991, it is notable that its growth rate has consistently exceeded that of the total population since 1961. The Statistics Canada projections envisage an impressive average 2.5+ percent per annum growth rate for the population aged 65 and older between 1971 and 1991. This is a level substantially above that projected for the total population.

2.4.2 Language and ethnic origin   Charts 2.7, 2.8 and 2.9 provide highly aggregated summary data on the trends in the composition of the population with respect to mother tongue, ethnic origin, and ability to speak the official languages of Canada. A recent slow decline in the percentage of the population with French mother tongue could possibly continue through 1991 (chart 2.7). The pattern of this projection is generally in line with that done by Henripin (1974, p. 15). The main beneficiary of the decline would be the proportion of the population with English as the mother tongue. ("Mother tongue" means the language first learned and still understood.) In general, as Canada becomes older as a country, and assuming no major and sustained upsurge of immigration, the combined proportions for English and French mother tongues will tend to increase as the percentage of native-born Canadians in the population grows.

Since the 1940s the proportion of British (English, Irish, Scottish, and Welsh) ethnic origin in the population has fallen slightly. The major increase has occurred in the group of Canadians who are of a European ethnic origin other than French. Chart 2.8 shows the relevant pattern.

From 1941 to 1971 the proportion of the population reporting an ethnic origin that is neither British nor European (including French) has grown from 2.3 percent to 3.7 percent. Despite serious defects in these data (see Henripin, 1974, pp. 39–41), these figures are probably reasonably accurate as regards the proportion of this "other ethnic origin" category in Canada's total population. If we were simply to double, as a hypothetical calculation, the 1961–71 increase in this share, and project the result forward to 1991, we would get only 5.7 percent of the Canadian population in the "other ethnic origin" group in 1991; but whether such doubling actually occurs in the future will depend on immigration policy. It should also be noted that in a number of Canadian communities the above-mentioned percentage is considerably higher than the national-level averages just cited.

Since 1951 there appears to have been a slight increase in the ability of Canadians to speak both official languages. According to the census data, the percentage of the population that is bilingual in French and English has grown from 12.3 percent in 1951 to 13.4 percent in 1971. A significant increase in this percentage is notable within each of the British, other European (excluding French), and the "other ethnic origin" groups.

21

Chart 2.7

**Historical and Projected Distribution
of the Population by Mother Tongue
Canada, 1951 to 1991**

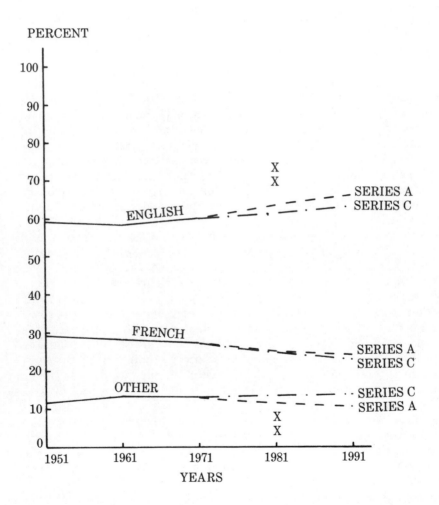

SOURCES: Statistics Canada, *1971 Census,* Cat. No. 92–725, Table 17; Cat.
No. 91–514, 1974.

Chart 2.8

Distribution of the Population by Ethnic Origin
Canada, 1941 to 1971

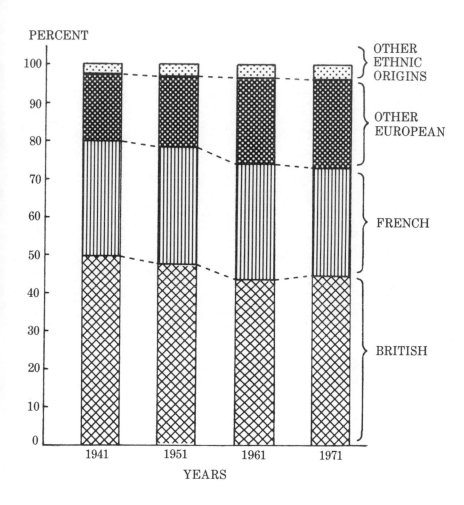

SOURCE: Statistics Canada, *1971 Census,* Cat. No. 92–723, Table 1.

Chart 2.9

Distribution by Official Language of the Populations in Selected Ethnic Origin Groups Canada, 1951 to 1971

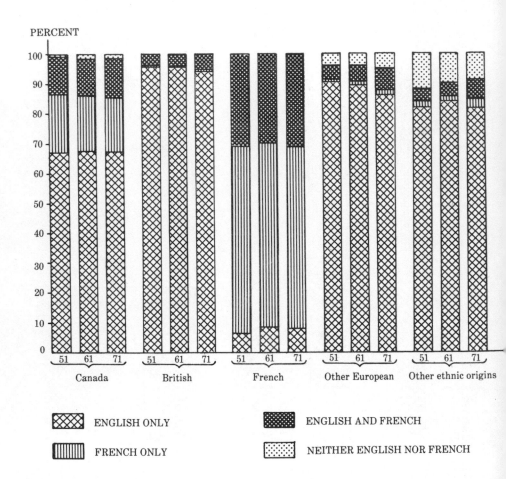

SOURCES: Statistics Canada, *1971 Census,* Cat. No. 92–736, Table 21. Dominion Bureau of Statistics, *1961 Census,* Vol. 1, Part 3, Table 120; *1951 Census,* Vol. 2, Table 45.

However, no group approaches the French ethnic origin group in ability to speak both official languages.

2.4.3 School enrolment and educational attainment   Consonant with the age distribution shifts already discussed, a plunge in enrolment levels at grades one to eight is envisaged through 1980–81. High school enrolment is projected as increasing through 1976, and declining thereafter.[4] Generally, slight increases in enrolment levels for the non-university post-secondary and for the university categories are projected. Compared to the estimated 1975–76 university enrolment of between 312,000 and 324,000 the percentage increase to 1985–86 is projected to be somewhere between 23 percent and 26 percent (see chart 2.10). However, the overall 1975–76 to 1985–86 university enrolment growth rate is substantially ahead of the projected population growth rate for persons aged 15 to 29.

As charts 2.11 and 2.12 show, the "quality" of the educational attainment mix of the Canadian population will continue to improve substantially under either projection alternative. By 1985, the number of persons who have completed university degrees is projected to lie somewhere between 1.99 million and 2.04 million, either figure implying a significant increase over 1.01 million, the estimated value for 1972. In other words, while population aged 20 and older (under Series A and Series C) is growing by at most 37 percent over the 1972 to 1986 period, the number of university graduates is growing by an impressive 90+ percent in that period. Over this same period the percentage with some university training in the population aged 14 and older is projected to rise from 14 percent to 19 percent among males, and from 9 percent to 12 percent among females.

These figures signal a wholly different level of "educational sophistication" in the Canadian population compared to that of 1951, when the percentage with some university training was 6 percent for males and 3 percent for females.

4.   Projections of school enrolment and educational attainment have recently been prepared by Dr. Zoltan Zsigmond and his colleagues (see Zsigmond and Rechnitzer, 1974). Dr. Zsigmond also made available an unpublished projection of the distribution of the population aged 14 and older by level of schooling. The figures presented below are transformations of his data in order to provide more adequate linkage of the figures to the Series A and Series C population projections. Chart 2.12 represents directly percentages provided by Dr. Zsigmond. (The title *non-university* in charts 2.11 and 2.12 refers to the post-secondary level. The title *complete non-university* in chart 2.12 pertains to persons who entered and successfully completed training in a non-university post-secondary institution.)

Chart 2.10

Historical and Projected School Enrolment
Canada, 1960–61 to 1985–86

(Series A)

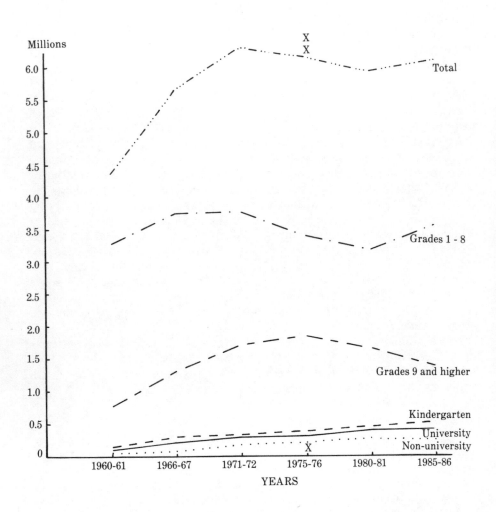

Chart 2.10 cont'd

Historical and Projected School Enrolment
Canada, 1960–61 to 1985–86

(Series C)

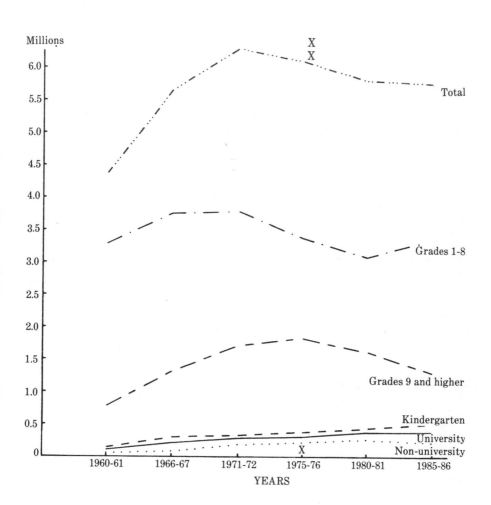

SOURCES: Zsigmond and Rechnitzer, 1974, Tables A–1 and A–2. Statistics Canada, Cat. No. 91–514, 1974, pp. 101–51.

Chart 2.11

Historical and Projected Population Aged 14 Years and Older
by Educational Attainment
Canada, 1951 to 1985

(Series A)

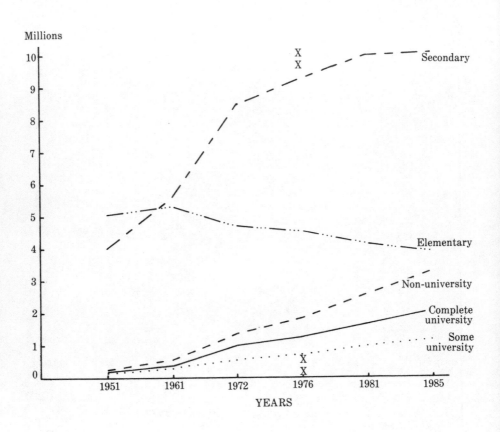

Chart 2.11 cont'd

Historical and Projected Population Aged 14 Years and Older
by Educational Attainment
Canada, 1951 to 1985

(Series C)

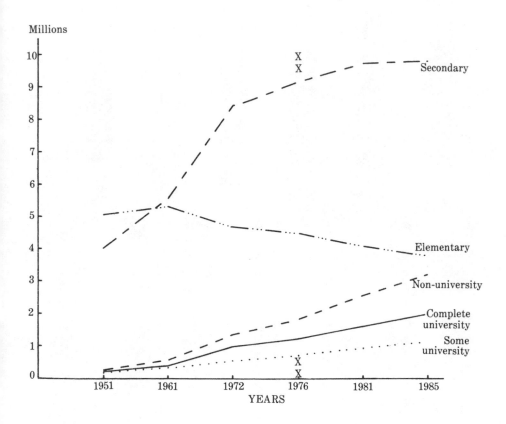

SOURCES: Zsigmond and Rechnitzer, 1974, Tables A–1 and A–2. Statistics Canada, Cat. No. 91–514, 1974, pp. 101–51.

Chart 2.12

Historical and Projected Distribution by Educational Attainment of the Population Aged 14 and Older
Canada, 1951 to 1985

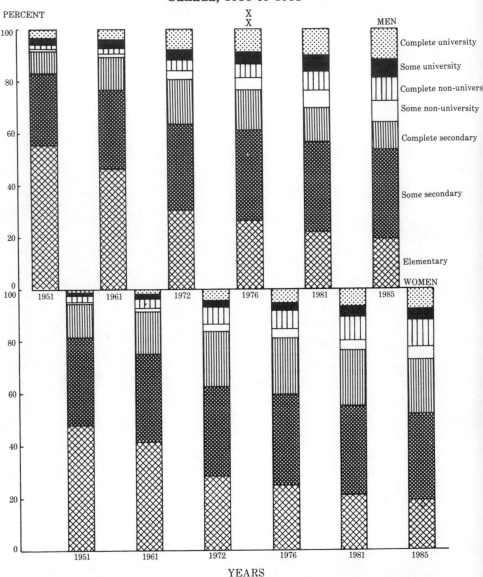

SOURCE: Unpublished projections prepared by Z. Zsigmond and E. Rechnitzer.

Chart 2.13

Historical and Projected Numbers of Families and Households
Canada, 1951 to 1991

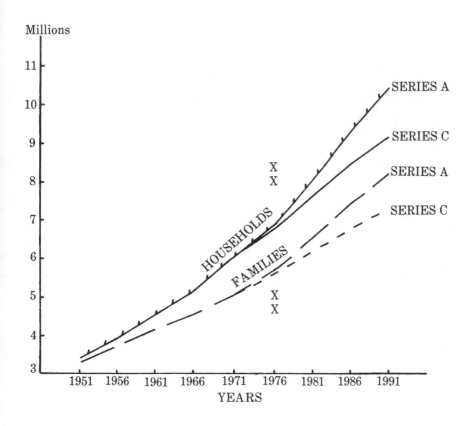

SOURCES: Kirkland, 1971, Tables 15 and 18. Statistics Canada, Cat. No. 91-514, 1974, pp. 101-51; *1971 Census,* Cat. No. 93-702, Table 1; *1971 Census,* Cat. No. 93-714, Table 1.

2.5 Families and Households

Strong rises are envisaged at least until 1991 in the numbers of households and families.[5] Between 1971 and 1981 household and family growth rates, as projected, are above population growth rates. Over this ten-year period at least 1.1 million additional families are envisaged in Canada, an increase of 22 percent since 1971. The corresponding increase in the number of households is 1.6 million, or 27 percent higher than the 1971 level. For both households and families, roughly one-half of these ten-year increases are projected to occur between 1971 and 1976 (see chart 2.13).

5. Projections previously published by John Kirkland and Systems Research Group form the basis of the data presented below with regard to families and households. A variety of recently available projections on these subjects were studied before choosing the work just mentioned.

3

PUBLIC POLICY ISSUES AND POPULATION TRENDS

3.1 Organization of the Discussion

Several important issues of public policy may be associated with Canadian population trends during the late 1970s and the 1980s. This chapter is a selective review of some of those issues. In order to organize the discussion, certain areas of population change are treated separately, though strong interconnections among such areas must be acknowledged. Short titles have been provided for each of the selected areas: population and labour force growth, geographic distribution and internal mobility, the older population, education of Canadians, and socio-cultural composition of population. Because the population processes, such as international migration, affect many of these fields, they will be brought into the discussion within several of the chapter sections below.

Although the emphasis below is on the anticipation of policy issues that will or should be debated during the next 15 years, no deliberate exclusion of currently important matters is made. A number of issues now of interest will continue to be so during the next 15 years, and it is fitting to give them some attention.

The commentary that follows is not intended to suggest conclusions concerning the relative priority or gravity of the identified issues within the context of the whole array of Canadian public policy problems. The authors do not wish to exaggerate the importance of population-related issues in Canada, although it must be admitted that the great focus on them in this volume may have the effect of over-emphasis in the mind of the reader.

Also it is not the authors' intention to suggest the most suitable form of approach to the resolution of policy issues for the public and its political representatives and servants, politicians and public officials.

3.2 National Population and Labour Force Growth

Population growth is directly related to several of the areas for public concern that will be discussed below. For example, changes in the geographic distribution of population result from regional differences in population growth rate. Changes in population composition result from growth rate differences among sub-groups of population. This section is concerned with changes in the size of the total national population, a growing focus of policy concern (see chapter four). In Canada policy issues concerning population growth are closely associated with those about the growth of the labour force. Accordingly, it seems worthwhile to treat the growth of the national population and labour force as an area for policy concerns.

Policy options that are intended to guide the growth of the total population or the labour force tend to deal directly with the immediate determinants (or components) of such growth: birth rates, death rates, migration rates, and labour force participation rates. Of major importance to birth rates are the rates of family formation and dissolution (nuptiality). Very closely connected with mortality are the processes of morbidity (disease and disability).

3.2.1 Boundaries   An area for policy concern, such as national population growth, is important partly because the variables that are pertinent to that area are strongly influential in the attainment of social welfare objectives. In some cases, the proper policy objective within a particular field is derived from pre-established aims in other fields. In other cases, the pursuit of a policy objective in a particular field requires concern for the constraints that the approach to that objective may place upon the attainment of aims in other fields. Population and labour force growth are no exceptions to these types of inter-field connection.

In short, the boundaries we draw around the field of population trends in the context of a discussion of public policy, are artificial. Similarly, the boundaries drawn about particular aspects of population trends are arbitrary and at best hazy, used only to help systematize the flow of discussion.

3.2.2 Population growth as a direct object of policy   Debate of policy issues that immediately involve growth of the Canadian population is by no means new. The history of such debate goes back at least to the 1950s, when the question of Canada's carrying capacity was discussed. Today the federal government appears to be encouraging Canadians to think explicitly about population growth and size as aspects of the determination of "what Canada wants" in the years ahead (see chapter four). Some explicit concern about the range within which Canada's population growth path should lie during the immediate and longer future does seem to be inevitable in mapping a network of Canadian social policy targets.

All populations must eventually reach an upper limit in size. However, there remains an important policy issue as to whether the attainment of that limit within an identifiable time frame will be actively sought.

There is a basic choice to be made between a policy of promoting stabilization of population size during the next 30 to 50 years and a policy of promoting continuous population growth during that period.

Significant policy questions on population growth rates in the near future will arise regardless of the choice that is made between the "stabilized size option" and the "continuous growth option". If the former option is chosen, what should be the desirable stable size and how soon do we want to reach that size? If the "continuous growth option" is chosen, then the desirable range for population growth rates in the near future should be determined, because the growth rate has substantial effects on some aspects of economic and social changes that are matters of concern to Canadians (see Economic Council of Canada, 1975a).

However, policy targets concerning the range of short-term *national* population growth rates do not comprise the most important aspect of growth policy to the majority of concerned citizens. For them the important aspect is the growth of the communities in which they expect to spend the better part of their lives. The distribution of growth among regions of Canada is an integral aspect of the problem of striking national objectives concerning population growth. Stated crudely, the basic query is: What is the desirable *distribution* of population growth among the different major regions and types of urban and rural areas? (See section 3.3 for discussion of this question.)

The importance of the shorter-term policies to guide population growth arises from the well-known fact that most social and economic problems and policies are significantly touched by changes in population size. This fact is already so embedded in Canadian policy-making work that an enumeration of examples seems superfluous. What should be signalled in this volume, in connection with the shorter-term growth management policies, is that there exists a task of deciding what can and should be done about major short-term fluctuations in growth that give rise to severe social and economic re-adjustment pressures. At least a policy of devotion of resources to the monitoring and wide reporting of the changes in reliable leading indicators of substantial fertility rate shifts, such as took place between 1957 and 1964, or of major alterations in population composition for certain communities caused by a geographic concentration of immigrants, may soon be debated in Canada.

3.2.3 Labour force growth   In developing policies in connection with population growth, Canadians need to pay close attention to the impact of population growth on the increase of the labour force. This matter has already been of concern in the federal and provincial policy spheres. Two of the significant policy questions in the field of labour force growth that can be identified at this time are:

1 What steps should be taken to ensure that labour force growth falls within a desirable range, if such a range is perceived to be needed to

help sustain *adequate rates of total national economic output* through the 1980s?

2 What steps should be taken to ensure that the geographic distribution of the labour force growth is consistent with policy objectives concerning the pattern of regional economic growth?

In regard to national economic growth, the foregoing remarks have stressed the total economic product rather than output per capita. The former has been judged in some literature to be a significant source of concern to policy-makers because growth of the total economic product is a significant factor in the capability of government to finance new or expanding social welfare programs. Some mention has also been made of the possible contribution of labour force growth to national income per capita; but the connection has not been clearly drawn. With regard to the above-mentioned balance in regional economic growth, the emphasis has been mainly on per capita income growth. In this context it is not so much the sheer amount of total labour force growth that has been indicated as relevant, but rather the growth of labour force sub-groups that have certain kinds of educational or occupational qualification.

The determination of the steps that will promote the desirable level of labour force growth presupposes a policy position as to where that level lies. It is assumed here that given prior determination of the desirable growth path for the total national economic product, the striking of consistent labour force growth rates is a technical research problem. To the extent that such research clearly indicates a particular range within which labour force growth ought to lie, in order to attain the economic growth objectives, then the range can be considered to have been a derived policy objective. (See Economic Council of Canada, 1975b, chap. 4.)

Another important problem in regard to labour force growth is to ensure that the relative rates of increase of workers in different occupational and educational groups will facilitate desired trends in the size and structure of the national economy. Some aspects of the educational attainment composition of new entrants to the labour force are discussed in section 3.4.2.

There is a temptation to regard labour force growth during the next 15 years as being largely insensitive to current or future policies since the population that will enter the force during this time period has already been born. However, policies can still affect near-term labour force growth through immigration and the labour force participation rates of certain substantial reservoirs of potential labour force growth (e.g. married women, young adults, and older adults). Policy issues that have ramifications for the labour force participation rates of females and older people are discussed in other sections below. (See also section 3.2.6 concerning immigration.)

The pace of labour force growth, due to new young adult entrants to the labour market, will likely decline, in comparison with recent years, the mid-1980s. If this eventuality is perceived to threaten the growth of national economic output that is required to finance Canadian social programs, then policies may soon need to be developed to promote improved contributions to labour force growth from other sources. (Some analysts contend that labour force growth is not the essential problem, but that the main difficulty is rather one of a "mis-match" between the compositions of labour demand and labour supply.)

3.2.4 Family formation and fertility Policy issues whose resolution has a significant bearing on population and labour force growth will be of continuing concern in the fields of family formation and human reproduction. The pressures to at least debate a policy option of widening freedom of choice in these fields will continue to grow in the years ahead. What is done to widen that freedom of choice could significantly affect the courses of population and labour force growth (through fertility and labour force participation rate changes). The above-mentioned debate may involve a re-examination of existing laws and regulations that touch on the ability to more effectively plan the number and timing of children by Canadian families (which will bring into consideration abortion and sterilization, and contraception), the ability to determine the grounds on which individuals can decide to form or dissolve families (which will involve divorce laws and regulations), and the legal implications of the formation or dissolution of a family unit.

3.2.5 Career opportunities for women One area in which the Canadian public and policy-makers will be drawn into a major debate that directly relates to the growth of the labour force, and more indirectly involves the future growth path of the national population, concerns the myriad of impediments that currently beset most women who wish to actively pursue dual in-the-home and out-of-home careers. There is a wide field of possible policy instruments that may contribute to the task of improving the freedom of choice of life goals for women in Canadian society—for example, the practices that govern entry into many occupations, institutional day care facilities for the children of women who wish to pursue out-of-home careers, the social organization of work (e.g. the degree of emphasis on full-time work) and the education of children that inhibit a more equitable distribution between husband and wife of the burdens of home maintenance, the availability of housing and related community services at reasonable cost, tax and welfare policies, and so on.

3.2.6 International migration Issues concerning international migration within the context of policy on population growth have been discussed from time to time in the history of Canada. Recently the government itself has offered an extended statement of options in the Green Paper on Immigration and a joint parliamentary committee has tabled pertinent recommendations (see chapter four). It would be superfluous to recount here the various policy issues that touch closely on immigration; but certain aspects of these issues ought to be mentioned.

With regard to the direct contribution of immigration to population growth, it should be noted that although new immigration legislation is imminent, it is unlikely that all relevant policy issues are about to be laid to rest. One reason for this statement lies in the nature of existing knowledge about emigration. No apparent attempt has been made in recent decades, at least, to measure directly the outflow of Canadians from Canada. We know relatively little about the magnitudes, fluctuations, and composition of emigration from Canada. If the fear grows that fertility rates will not be high enough to prevent the onset of absolute decline in the population, or if the concern to keep out would-be immigrants of certain cultural backgrounds reaches a fever pitch, we may well see an upsurge of interest in the control of emigration. At least, the issue of whether emigration ought to be monitored more systematically than at present might become more urgent.

Another issue that the forthcoming legislation will not solve for long is the extent to which immigration policy should help resolve perceived supply bottlenecks or surpluses in Canadian labour markets. As the cohort of the recent baby depression of the 1960s and 1970s reaches young adulthood, labour force growth may well come under strong dampening influence from purely demographic factors, and the tailoring of immigration to meet labour market needs may again become a matter of major policy concern.

Implemented immigration regulations will not easily satisfy the widely varying kinds of policy objective with respect to which immigration is currently being viewed as a potentially handy tool. These include guidance of population growth, matching labour supply with labour demand, humanitarian re-uniting of families or accommodation of refugees, among others (see Canada, Manpower and Immigration, 1974a). A significant continuing policy problem will be that of striking an appropriate compromise among these types of objective. The compromise that is struck at any given time will depend on the then prevailing circumstances and political pressures. Thus it will be under close scrutiny and pressure as circumstances change—in short, immigration will recurrently be a source of significant public policy issues in the future. Indeed, the essence of this remark was confirmed in testimony by the Honourable Robert Andras to the Special Joint Committee on Immigration Policy:

Immigration in my view should be seen essentially as the mechanism to support whatever demographic goals may from time to time be determined. The act I think therefore need not, and indeed perhaps should not, itself attempt to spell out such matters as the numbers of people who should be admitted as immigrants or the precise techniques which might be employed to effect the better distribution of the immigration flow among regions in Canada. But such a new act could well require the government to determine the volume of immigration in conformity with a population policy and the objectives of that policy, as these emerge in the light of conditions which I think by necessity will be changing and will be dynamic and will not be carved in stone at any given time. (Canada, Parliament, Special Joint Committee of the Senate and of the House of Commons on Immigration Policy, 9 April 1975a, p. 10.)

3.2.7 Summary   In summary, it would seem that as Canadians become increasingly concerned about aspects of the character of life in their communities that do not directly involve wealth and income, the notion will be more widely accepted that some basic policy position must be taken about the desirable range of population growth in the near-term. Basic positions must also be established about the desirable range of labour force growth during the next 15 years, at least if this is considered necessary to sustain desirable levels of economic growth, assuming that the attainment of such economic growth is seen to be a *sine qua non* of effective pursuit of the network of social welfare policies that is already in place.

Policy options aimed at an expansion of the freedom of choice of family members, especially women but also men, to pursue dual in-the-home and out-of-home careers will become increasingly pressing during the next 15 years. Implementation of such options could bear substantial consequences for both population and labour force growth. Some of the fields of policy endeavour that are involved include aspects of reproductive behaviour (e.g. contraception, abortion, and sterilization), of family formation and dissolution (e.g. divorce and marriage laws), of the organization of paid work with respect to the in-the-home responsibilities of family members, and of the nature of the "male" and "female" roles that children are taught.

International migration as an avenue for policy levers to guide population and labour force growth will not cease to be a major area of concern, even if new immigration legislation is passed in the near future. Policy on the interconnection of the volume of annual immigration with labour market conditions will become necessary if lagging labour force growth from internal sources becomes apparent in the 1980s and is widely deemed to be undesirable. The issue of monitoring and even controlling the annual rate of emigration from Canada will grow in importance.

3.3 Geographic Redistribution Trends

3.3.1 Scope of the field   The allocation of the national population among defined geographic areas is the usual meaning of the concept *population distribution.* Changes in the pattern of that allocation are the immediate consequences of differences in regional growth rates. The regional growth rate differences are in turn outcomes of the same demographic processes, operating at the regional level, that were mentioned in section 3.2 concerning national population growth—mortality, fertility, and migration (geographic mobility).

A variety of regional systems are relevant to a discussion on population distribution. In this volume emphasis is placed on provinces, rural and urban areas, metropolitan areas, and broad sub-provincial economic regions (e.g. the northwestern region of Ontario, or the Gaspé region of Quebec). With regard to the demographic processes, particular attention is placed on geographic mobility, since it is traditionally the most important source of population redistribution among regions in Canada.

As in the case of national population growth (discussed in section 3.2), there are important interconnections between public policies in the field of population distribution and in other fields. The connections in some cases can be such as to cause policy-makers to derive the population distribution policies from objectives embraced in regard to aspects of social and/or economic policy.

Before outlining some of the central policy issues regarding the distribution of population, it is desirable to indicate the meaning that will be given in this volume to one concept that will frequently be used—*distribution policy.* (The reader may recall the discussion of the concept of population distribution in section 1.1.) The term, distribution policy, is really a shorthand reference to a wide range of policies that touch on different aspects of population distribution. Thus the concept of distribution policy does not pertain to a single policy, but rather to a collection of policies.

3.3.2 Urban policies and intergovernmental collaboration   Rapid pace of urbanization and policies that tend to favour urban growth for its own sake are largely *passé* in Canada. With the decline of the "growth is good" syndrome, policies about urban communities will increasingly involve issues concerning the quality of urban life. In the context of these issues slow growth or even stagnation (in some communities) may be assumed (see Lithwick, 1970, chap. 5). A pertinent area of concern is the organization of intergovernmental relations to provide for more extensive recycling of tax revenues, collected by "senior" levels of government, to the municipal level. This would improve the opportunity for local financing of urban services in areas such as recreation, public utility facilities, waste disposal, transportation, and law enforcement.

3.3.3 Metropolitan area growth   Some of the most fundamental and difficult policy issues that Canadians will continue debating are related to the recent rapid growth of a handful of metropolitan areas, to the concentration of the national population into these areas, and to the redistribution of population and economic activity away from the core cities and towards the outer parts of metropolitan areas. The following comments highlight some of the enduring policy issues that relate to these two features of the urbanization of Canada in the 1960s and 1970s.

Are the forces that will mould the future metropolitan growth in Canada (both demographic and non-demographic aspects) to include deliberate "growth-guiding" policies by the pertinent levels of Canadian government acting in collaboration? The federal government has apparently recognized this question to be among the forefront of the significant policy issues that face Canadians at present and in the near future, and a policy position has already been established in the process of tri-level intergovernmental consultations (see chapter four). If an effective growth-guiding policy can be implemented with respect to metropolitan areas it may have substantial impact on the pattern of regional economic growth, the rate at which a few urban centres garner major political influence, and threaten to become virtual city-states within Canada, the degree to which environmental quality problems in the metropolitan areas (including housing, traffic and communication congestion, waste disposal, water and air quality) can be adequately managed, and the rate at which social problems such as crime and inter-group conflicts will grow in the country. Studies sponsored by Canadian governmental authorities have already called attention to some of the implications of various aspects of the "metropolitanization trend" and pointed to the need for policy initiatives (Economic Council of Canada, 1967, p. 267; Lithwick, 1970, pp. 125–36; Task Force on Housing and Urban Development, 1969, p. 195; Science Council, 1975).

3.3.4 The city-state issue   One aspect of the metropolitanization trend could assume major proportions as a ground for public debate. Metropolitan areas are natural reservoirs of political power. If this power is organized and mobilized in such a way as to press the issue of a proper voice for urban population concentrations in policy deliberations that integrally involve their interests, should structural rearrangements be made in the Canadian political system in order to enable this voice to be heard in a satisfactory manner? Already there are some who contend that metropolitan areas such as Montreal, Toronto, and Vancouver have earned the right to be treated more extensively as quasi-independent units that could deal directly with the federal level of government.

3.3.5 Metropolitan housing, crime, inter-group conflicts, and transportation   The growing metropolitanization of Canada directly affects the gravity of social problems that will exercise Canadians in the years ahead. Four problems that are important grounds for policy issues are especially worthy of note in this context—the adequate supply of low-priced housing, the incidence of crimes, the potential for overt inter-group conflicts within metropolitan areas, and the adequacy of transportation. These grounds for major policy issues are partly inter-related, they are dependent to some degree on the performance of the economy, and Canadians have already started to debate them. Only a few central policy issues will be mentioned in passing here, since much has already been written about these areas.

The sheer availability of housing at prices that can comfortably be met by lower income groups has become a much discussed problem in several of Canada's urban centres. If it can be assumed that no sustained economic boom or reallocation of existing tax revenues will soon generate public funds on the scale needed to subsidize a substantial lowering of housing prices, then this problem may not disappear in the near-term. A central issue here is the following. What is the responsibility of government to intervene in the operation of "free market" forces in order to help increase the supply of housing at prices that lower income families can adequately manage, and what steps should the different spheres of Canadian government (acting in concert) take to break the price squeeze? This issue is already considerably exercising Canadian governments, and a number of policy initiatives aimed at improving the supply of modestly priced housing have been announced.

In connection with this brief comment on housing policy issues, it is worthwhile to mention a relatively recent significant development in the field of household and family formation that helps to impart an impetus to the demand for housing units. This development is the steady rise in the numbers and proportion of one-person and non-family households. The trend is particularly notable in metropolitan areas where income levels and lifestyles are most conducive to its manifestation.

The growing metropolitanization of Canada involves factors that tend to weaken the forces of informal social control over the incidence of crime. The net effect of this weakening is to place greatly increased pressure on the formal institutions for social control (law enforcement agencies). A central policy issue (in connection with crime) will develop in the face of the spread of crime in urban centres. What is the responsibility of government to try to counteract the breakdown of informal social control mechanisms by such possible measures as promoting the development of neighbourhood and local community organizations and associations whose activities can support those of formal law enforcement agencies?

Economic problems, especially in the fields of jobs and housing, together with the juxtaposition of a variety of sub-cultures within Canada's metropolitan areas, have created a heightened potential for overt inter-group conflicts in this country. Several policy issues are raised in this connection, some of which are mentioned in section 3.4.

Transportation problems are exacerbated by the growth of large metropolitan areas, especially lateral growth, although growth *per se* is only one of the elements involved in explaining the rise of such problems. The dimensions of these problems and the policy issues they pose have been the subjects of literature and public debate (see e.g. Reynolds, 1971; and Municipality of Metropolitan Toronto, 1975). Questions of integrating intra-metropolitan transportation system improvements with land and neighbourhood conservation (and/or development) objectives, of development of new transportation technologies, and of financing such development, will continue to be grounds for public debate in the years ahead. Another dimension of transportation problems involves the heavy concentration of urban and metropolitan development in the Windsor–Quebec City corridor. Partly because of the population concentration in this area, demands for efficient inter-city transportation may expand substantially, and policies to meet these demands will continue to be debated.

3.3.6 Intra-metropolitan redistribution   Within individual metropolitan areas, an explosion of "suburban" growth has been accompanied by much slower increase in central-city populations. The suburbanization trend has at least two important components: (1) the size and growth of the suburban population, and (2) expansion of the territory or "urban occupancy" close to the centres of major urban agglomerations. The degree and manner in which the "behaviour" of these variables is to be guided by governments in the future make up an important issue within the scope of distribution policies. Since much literature has been written about the problems associated with the intra-metropolitan redistribution of the population and economy in North America, no elaboration will be attempted in this volume. Suffice it to mention in passing four policy issues that will continue to exercise Canadians:

1 What steps should governments take to improve orderly geographic expansion of metropolitan areas so as to conserve vital agricultural land and provide reasonable access by a wide spectrum of Canadians to recreational properties in the hinterland of metropolises?
2 How much and in what ways will tax revenues collected in the federal and provincial spheres of government be recycled back, to the extent needed, to metropolitan communities to help counteract the tendency towards obsolescence and decay in the cores of major cities and help finance the maintenance and improvement of social services and amenities in those city cores?
3 Should policies that promote increased density of population about specific sub-centres within metropolitan areas be adopted in order to

ease the logistical and cost problems of delivering social services and transportation facilities to metropolitan populations?

4 Should governments promote and help to finance the establishment of growth centres and/or new towns within the orbits of metropolises?

3.3.7 Balanced regional growth Significantly related to metropolitan growth in Canada, through the pattern of geographic concentration of metropolitan areas, is the problem of attaining policy objectives regarding balanced regional economic growth. Concern with the regional pattern of economic growth has been a major aspect of Canadian government policies in recent decades, and much has been written about this matter. Two relevant sets of issues may be mentioned briefly, since they will continue to be of importance to policy-makers in the future. The geographic distribution of population is an important factor in dealing with these sets of issues.

The recent trends in the redistribution of the national population among the provinces are increasingly exercising politicians (see chapter four) for reasons that involve purely political as well as economic considerations. Projection of these trends indicates substantial population gains for some provinces and significant losses for others. In some circles policies that may help to maintain the current provincial percentage distribution of the national population are being debated. Two issues that will increasingly be raised are whether and how governments should try to intervene in the process of interprovincial population redistribution, and whether the costs of such intervention will be acceptable to Canadians.

Another aspect of regional growth policy is that of improving the economic viability of certain regions that are perceived to be suffering from lagging growth due to the "natural market forces." The Department of Regional Economic Expansion (DREE) has been active in this area, and much related literature has been written. Here it is sufficient to mention three central issues related to the problem:

1 What is the proper balance between efforts to rebuild and sustain a buoyant economy in lagging regions, to help them retain their shares of the national population, and efforts to facilitate net out-migration of "surplus" labour from such regions?
2 If the relatively small-scale industrial incentives and infra-structure support programs of DREE are judged to be largely ineffective by the key public(s) and politicians, what substitute government initiatives can be undertaken at acceptable costs on behalf of lagging regions?
3 To what extent should governments subsidize the delivery of services to the population that elects to remain in lagging economic regions, as well as help finance the upgrading or changing of skills among the working force of such areas?

3.3.8 Mobility policy issues   Related to all the previous issues in the field of population distribution are the demographic mechanisms embodied in redistribution processes. These mechanisms involve internal migration, external migration, and regional differences in natural increase (births minus deaths) rates. In this discussion attention is concentrated mainly on migration since it is more of a target of policy initiatives than is natural increase. Government actions aimed at guiding or facilitating both types of migration (internal and external) form a major aspect of distribution policies.

One thing common to both types of migration in Canada is that internal migrants and immigrants favour metropolitan centres as areas of destination. Based on the 1971 Census, the largest five-year (1966–1971) internal migration flows among municipalities involved metropolitan areas (at both origin and destination). Persons moving from non-metropolitan to metropolitan areas made up another substantial block of all intermunicipal migrants. A clear preference for metropolitan areas by immigrants is also shown in the available data. For example, the vast majority of the persons who established residence in Canada between 1966 and 1971 chose to live in metropolitan areas.

One general policy issue which arises from the foregoing discussion is whether and how governments should attempt to influence the pattern and momentum of the major internal, as well as the external migration flows. This issue embodies a number of subsidiary matters such as incentives towards altering the overwhelming concentration of immigrants in just a few of the metropolitan areas, inducements towards settlement of immigrants and internal migrants in selected parts of non-metropolitan areas (or territory near to such areas), and increasing the attractiveness of smaller centres (including new towns and centres outside the immediate zones of influences of metropolitan areas) to internal migrants and immigrants.

Another important subsidiary matter relates to the control over the flow of external migration. At various times in the past, immigration policy has dealt both with the number of people admitted to Canada and their areas of settlement within Canada. In future the distributional aspect of immigration policy will receive careful attention, since this matter could significantly affect the balance of growth among regions (especially if regional birth rates converge towards very low levels). Although policy instruments aimed at directly influencing the regional distribution of emigration may not be feasible, knowledge about this distribution will be relevant to the development of the distributional aspect of immigration policy. Whether immigrants should be coerced or induced into settling outside certain metropolitan areas is already a debated issue, and it may not be resolved soon.

Manpower objectives regarding investment in human resources and attempts to improve the balance between the locations of jobs and people qualified to hold them also involve policies on geographic mobility. One aspect of manpower mobility policies which has received significant discussion is the desirability of instituting measures that will enhance the level of population mobility. It has been thought that a variety of adjustments to changes in the economy can be accomplished more smoothly with enhanced levels of population mobility. For example, it has been held in some circles that the levels of out-migration from relatively depressed regions have been too low.

3.3.9 Integration of national and regional growth policies   A given growth rate of the national population could coincide with several different distributional patterns. Thus an action aimed at influencing the overall growth rate of national population is not (without elaboration) an instrument of distribution policy. However, a policy on growth becomes such an instrument to the degree that the process of attaining a given national growth rate is meant to be accompanied by a tendency towards a specific pattern among the component regional growth rates. Whether the accompaniment of a specific regional pattern of growth rates, if planned, can be achieved is a matter that requires careful consideration in the integration of national and regional growth policies. It would be desirable to address the range of alternative regional growth patterns that would be consistent with the attainment of particular national population growth objectives.

3.3.10 Summary   In summary of this selective review of central issues that will face Canadians in the next 15 years in connection with the geographic distribution of population, it may be noted that most of the highlighted issues have already emerged on the stage of public debate and political concern. However, much more debate of these issues can be expected. For the purposes of quick recollection, a list of over-simplified titles of the highlighted issues may be provided: improvement in the quality of urban life and services; explicit policies to guide metropolitan growth; the rise of the metropolitan city-state; adequate supply of housing at low cost; the breakdown of the informal forces of social control with respect to crimes; the potential for overt inter-group conflicts; adequacy of transportation; conservation of vital agricultural and recreational lands; retarding physical decay and deterioration of social services in central city cores; increase of intra-metropolitan densities in order to facilitate the delivery of social services and transportation facilities; major shifts in provincial shares of the national population; the viability of regions of "lagging" economic growth; the scope for and acceptability of efficacious inducements to internal mobility of population and the settlement pattern of immigrants; the commitment to increased mobility as an avenue towards more equitable access to personal growth opportunities; and the integration of regional and national population growth objectives.

3.4 Changes in Population Composition

3.4.1 Attributes selected for emphasis   In section 3.3 it was noted that a concern with population distribution was not separate from one with growth. Concern with the former was merely a question of concentrating on some aspects of the manifestations of regional growth differences. Growth differences are again involved when we treat the field of trends in the composition of population. Important sub-groups of the population may be identified in terms of selected categories of attributes such as sex, age, languages currently spoken, mother tongue, ethnic origin, marital status, and educational attainment. Shifts in the proportional representation of the important population sub-groups (compositional changes) are significant sources of social problems and related public policy concerns. Intrinsic to the field of compositional trends as an area for public policy concern is the pattern of variation among sub-groups with respect to the population processes, particularly fertility, nuptiality, mortality, morbidity, labour force participation, and schooling participation.

A great variety of composition attributes and population sub-groups could be covered in the discussion that follows. Based on the literature and the experts consulted in developing this report, the following "composition dimensions" were selected for emphasis: age, education, language, and ethnic origin. With respect to each of these attributes population processes have or will engender changes that give rise to, or exacerbate, social problems which in turn raise important concerns in the field of public policy.

The general caution mentioned in sections 3.2 and 3.3 concerning interconnections among objectives from different policy fields also applies to changes in population composition. Frequently, for example, policy objectives concerning some aspects of composition are derived from matters involving social welfare and cultural change in Canada.

3.4.2 Education   Future public policy ramifications of population trends arise both from the character of such trends in the years ahead, and from the unfolding effects of past trends. Age composition change is an area where past population trends in Canada embody important public policy consequences that have yet to be fully unfolded. The unprecedented fall of the birth rate since the late 1950s, following the significant rise in the post-war baby boom, has led directly to a steady increase in the proportion of adults in the population. The proportion of older adults, in particular, has been rising steadily though not dramatically since the early 1960s.

A great variety of social and economic consequences and problems are arising partly from the changing age composition of the Canadian population. A report much longer than the present one could be confined to this topic alone, since the consequences touch such a wide spectrum of areas—dependency, labour force mobility and productivity, adequacy of self-generated personal incomes (especially retirement incomes), the burden of health care, technological innovations in housing and related community services, the volume and composition of demand for education, and the practices and rules concerning retirement from the labour market. The literature and experts consulted in developing this report suggested two areas of important consequences of age distributional change in Canada that should be chosen for emphasis. The first is education and the second is the welfare of the older population, and both are major contributors to the size of the society's "welfare budget." This section will concentrate on education and the following one will deal with the older population.

The massive growth of the child population that followed the Second World War and the partly coincident major increase in the technological sophistication of the Canadian economy have been partly responsible for a substantial expansion of the "education industry" in Canada. All branches of education have been involved, highlighted by a spectacular explosion of the demand and supply of post-secondary education in the 1960s. The increase in the costs to taxpayers of developing and maintaining the education industry was also striking, and it became apparent that the growth curve of education system costs was on an upward path that would probably be unsustainable in Canada.

Tax pressures associated with the financing of the education industry, and the increasing doubt in the value of continuing the societal devotion to the growth of this industry that was marked by the 1960s, are a partial source of significant public policy issues in the field of education. Recent population trends are another important partial source of such issues. The massive decline of the birth rate, starting in the late 1950s and continuing for more than a decade, has initially dampened the growth rate of demand for elementary education.

In future it will exert a dampening influence on the demand for secondary and then university education. For example, only a new expansiveness in the taste for long-duration post-secondary education by young adults, and/or a substantial rise in the demand for retraining and education for aging and leisure on the part of the middle-aged and older population, can help to avoid a substantial flattening of the growth curve of university enrolments in the mid-1980s.

The problems posed by the population trends for education policies in Canada are also partly dependent on the massive human and non-human capital investments that have slowly been put in place to meet surging demand in particular sectors of the industry. There is a wrenching process of individual and social readjustment when the character of the demand shifts, and this is partly a result of population trends.

In short, Canadian education is a field of public policy concern to which demographic trends are quite relevant. As in so many other areas, the issues and the related societal problems do not stem from population trends alone; but these trends comprise one of the important sources of the public policy issues in the field of education that will continue to face Canada during the next 15 years.

Most of the important public issues related to the education of Canadians have been raised and publicly debated, and in greater or lesser degrees they are attracting substantial attention from the relevant Canadian governments. It is sufficient in this volume to highlight some of the issues that will continue to be significant in the near future or will emerge to be of importance in the 1980s.

In the light of their major drain on tax revenues, the productivity of the resources made available to the education industry has become a prominent ground for public debate and policy issues in Canada. Partly because teachers at all levels are becoming more organized to protect what they perceive to be their right to adequate working conditions and a more active role in the determination of education policy, this debate will not end soon. Indeed it will become more heated in the near future, because the "unionization" of the teachers will have the effect of placing a growing constraint on the governments' capability to quickly reduce the growth rate of costs in the education industry. Some central policy questions may be posed in this context. What instruments should be brought to bear upon the problem of improving productivity in the education industry to help control the growth rate of costs? Can they simultaneously maintain the adequacy of the services provided to pupils and afford the room that teachers perceive they need to protect desirable working conditions?

Among the important subsidiary questions to the one just mentioned is the use of the physical plant of the education industry at times when it is not occupied in the process of delivering services to students. What steps should be taken by the pertinent governments to expand the use of the plant of the education industry, especially during times when it would otherwise be idle? Also, what initiatives should be taken to promote the design of new facilities in the plant of the education industry so that when those facilities tend to become unused because of demographic and other changes (such as the decline in the size of the population demanding services at the elementary level) they can be more readily adapted to alternative uses?

Flexibility as regards future changes in the composition of education services provided to the population has already become an important issue and will be more so in the future. Because of demographic and economic changes, the composition of demand for education services can and has undergone major alterations. We are witnessing at present a substantial relative decline in the demand for elementary education. Later in the century, we may witness a substantial relative advance in the demand for education among the middle-aged and older population.

The possible adjustments to shifts in the composition of demand for educational services go beyond the matters of specialization in the non-human resources available to the industry and matters of curriculum design. They also significantly involve the job mobility of persons who are initially trained to be teachers in certain sectors of the education industry. Adequacy of basic education and experience to permit teachers to change jobs smoothly is a growing problem. It will soon confront' a substantial proportion of those specializing in high school education, and later in the 1980s university teachers, on a large scale, will have to grapple with it. This problem of flexibility confronts the educational system; but because these matters are so potentially under the control of Canadian governments there is clearly room for debate of public policies related to the flexibility of the education industry.

The growing unionization of teachers as an occupational group which has recently manifested itself in increased militancy raises some substantial public policy issues that will be vigorously debated in the 1970s and 1980s. Among these issues is the question of the degree to which the public and governments should tolerate, without substantial sanctions, long strikes or other efforts at major withdrawal of services by groups of teachers in such a way as to crucially affect the rate of social maturation and education of children in the nation's communities.

The number of school leavers with university education is projected to continue growing substantially until the early 1980s. It has been suggested that by the 1980s labour markets may make a decreasing distinction between degree holders and others with less academic qualification—indeed the process of devaluing the university degree as an automatic key to good jobs is already underway. If this suggestion is correct, a substantial number of university graduates will face a problem of transition to a labour market in which the intellectual challenge of work is far below that of being at school and the ostensible economic value of the degree is not highly visible. Whether the problem is perceived to be serious or even catastrophic in its scope will depend on the expectations that the graduates carry into the labour market. A substantial issue in the field of educational policy will be whether government should help to restructure the identified goals of higher education thereby helping to reduce the number of graduates entering the labour market with unduly inflated expectations. The problem of restructuring those goals is in the first instance that of the educational system itself; but so pervasive is the influence of governments over this system that the problem should also be viewed as one that faces public policy-makers. One area, for example, of potential influence is that of policies concerning the relative growth of university and community college facilities.

As the decline continues in the notions that there are important differential income returns to university education, and that major support of such education is required to help fuel Canadian economic growth, the rationale for massive financing of university education from public revenues will increasingly be called into question. Public policy-makers will be under great pressure to decide what level of allocation of tax revenues to the subsidization of university education is appropriate, and politically acceptable. An important reason for this pressure will be the growing claim of other uses, such as services on behalf of the older population, upon the fund of tax revenues.

Important changes in the character of Canadian society and in Canadian culture will continue to flow from the continuing increase in the proportion of well-educated persons in the population. Among the policy issues that will be accentuated by this process is that of providing acceptable avenues for concerned groups to make inputs to the formulation of public policy issues and to deliberations about their solutions. An increasingly educated population will make growing demands for more effective public inputs to and participation in on-going political processes, beyond that of the regular election of political representatives.

3.4.3 Canada's older population   Among the population sub-groups that form important political constituencies and suffer from a wide variety of disadvantages that social policies have been devised to alleviate, probably none will be more prominent in Canada during the next 15 years than the older population. This statement seems reasonable even though the "older population explosion" will occur in the next century. For the purposes of this section we may identify this population as being composed of those who are approaching or have passed the mean age of retirement from the labour market for their sex (roughly, age 60 for females and age 65 for males). The older population has been growing more rapidly than the total national population for most of the last 15 years and has already assumed a formidable absolute size. This is a population whose dependency on ameliorative welfare policies covers a wide variety of aspects of social life (employment opportunity, health, housing, recreation, community services, education, etc.) and consumes a large segment of the national welfare budget.

The growth of the older population sharpens two overriding policy issues. Firstly, what is the extent of the responsibility of government to provide and finance, where necessary, the services and facilities needed by the older population, and how can the potentially enormous cost of meeting this responsibility be rendered acceptable to the rest of the Canadian population (especially those who are contributing out of their current earnings a major portion of the above-mentioned financing)? Secondly, in view of the fact that all levels of Canadian governments are becoming or have become engaged in the development and implementation of social policies on behalf of the older population, what governmental structures and collaborative functions must be developed and implemented in order to ensure that an integrated network of social policies is evolved to conserve the resources that the society spends in this general area? Both of these questions are already exercising Canadian governments, and it is virtually certain that they will become more important in the years ahead.

Near the centrepiece of social policy concerning the older population is the problem of adequacy of income. In most cases private savings accumulated by an older person while he or she was earning income will be far from adequate. Already there are rumblings to the effect that private and public pension programs as presently constituted and funded will not be able to cope with the demand upon them that the older population will raise in the years ahead. Since with sufficient income an older person could take some reasonably effective steps to obtain necessary services in such areas as housing, health care, and recreation, it is apparent that the inadequacy of accumulated private savings and pensions will lead, and it already has led, to great pressure upon governments to provide income support. Will the income maintenance programs currently in place be adequate to meet the needs of Canada's older population through the remainder of the present century? If not, what is the responsibility of government to improve these programs and can the cost of such improvements be rendered acceptable to the great bulk of the Canadian electorate?

In addition to income transfer programs, there are a number of areas in which policies may be instituted to ease the problem of adequacy of income among the older population. These areas include the laws and regulations concerning the age of retirement, the differences among industries and occupations in regard to the provisions and benefits of pension programs, and regulations concerning income tax deductions.

An issue that will have to be faced in the expansion of income-transfer programs is that of the integration of transfer schemes aimed at the older population with those aimed at other disadvantaged groups in such a way that perceived inequities do not become a source of disturbing political confrontation, particularly among age groups. A confrontation among age groups may already be brewing in regard to the regulations and practices concerning the age of retirement and the manner in which work activities are organized in the light of the age differences in physical abilities (at least). For many years it has been popular to support lowering of the age of retirement. As the older population becomes a larger proportion of the electorate in Canada, governments may well be faced with a strong demand to reverse the popular practices and provide more widespread opportunities for older workers to continue working beyond the current mean age of retirement if they care to do so. Also policies will be debated concerning the technical and physical requirements involved in work activities undertaken by older people, the recruitment practices of employers, and the education and retraining of older workers to facilitate their occupational mobility.

The field of health care is another in which the costs of supporting a much larger older population, and one of growing sophistication in terms of its demands upon politicians, could be staggering, compared to historical precedents in this country. In this traditionally youth-dominated society, persons concerned with health care programs, facilities, and personnel have only recently begun to think seriously about the reorganization and reallocation of services that will be implied by a shift to an old-age oriented society. We have only to look at the emphasis on hospitalization facilities provided for acute illnesses to begin to visualize the pressures that could be placed upon health care systems in Canada from a growing older population. Public policy-makers will have to grapple with the issues of the expansion of education concerning the processes and problems of individual aging, of major restructuring of the content of the training provided to those occupations that provide health care services, and of the reallocation of the resources that are made available to provide fixed capital in the health care industry.

Special problems also arise in the field of housing. Governments will have to face more vigorously the question of the steps that need to be taken to promote innovations in housing design and in related community services and transportation to facilitate the meeting of individual problems of older people.

The great variety of policy issues that arise in this connection, and indeed in connection with the other areas of problems of an older population mentioned above, have been the subject of substantial Senate inquiries and conferences in Canada. The volume of world literature in this area is large and growing rapidly. Accordingly, it is not worthwhile to elaborate much further upon the subject, except to emphasize the significance to the character of Canadian society of the shift from a youth to an old-age oriented culture.

3.4.4 Language and ethnic origin   Inter-group differences in the rates of population processes, particularly fertility and international migration, have entailed inter-group variation in growth rates that can aggravate social problems. However, they can also contribute to beneficial cultural variety. Prominent among the pertinent population trends in this context are the recent fall in the proportion of the Canadian population that is predominantly French-speaking, the unusually rapid growth of the native Indian population, and the higher than average growth rate of the population whose ethnic origin is neither British nor French.

So much has been written and debated on the subject of linguistic equality and language rights in Canada, and the central problems in this area have so clearly been big concerns of Canadian governments, that there is little to be said in this volume that can hope to be a significant addition to existing general knowledge. However, we can signal some demographic changes that will likely bear substantial ramifications for public policy in the field of language. Firstly, a trend of decline in the proportion of the national population that is either of French mother tongue or which predominantly speaks French appears to be underway. In Quebec the provincial government is already actively developing policies intended to protect French-Canadian institutions, language, and culture. At the federal level, and among other provincial governments, policy steps intended to ensure the language rights of predominantly French-speaking minorities outside Quebec will be the subject of continuing debate about the appropriate means to be used. Perceived declines in the political weight of French Canadians and Quebec in national government policy-making, partly as a result of the demographic trends just mentioned, will be the basis of substantial debates in the future.

Some analysts contend that even if the proportional weight of French Canadians in the total national population can be stabilized in the future, trends in the geographic redistribution of linguistic groups and in language assimilation processes are threatening the eventual substantial decline in the relative numbers of French-speaking minorities outside Quebec (see Joy, 1967; Maheu, 1970; Henripin, 1974) and of English-speaking minorities inside Quebec (see Joy, 1967). As these developments, if they materialize more clearly, become more generally visible, policy-makers and the public will be confronted with the issue of their desirability for the long-term integrity of Canada. A policy position would then have to be taken as to whether efforts should be made to halt the trends.

Immigration, family planning, practices concerning the use of French language in work, and promotion of aspects of French-Canadian culture are among the principal avenues being pursued or discussed with the objective of retarding the diminution of the weight of French Canada in the life of the nation. A number of issues connected with the appropriateness and effectiveness of specific policy initiatives are already being debated and this will continue in the years ahead.

Canada's native Indian population has been growing substantially faster than the total national population. There is a continuing process of up-grading in the levels of education among Canadian Indians. A number of significant policy issues will be reinforced by these trends. Three of these issues can be listed as follows:

1 What is the responsibility of Canadian governments to help promote an adequate supply of employment and local economic development opportunities to meet the needs of the growing populations of Indian and Inuit descent?

2 Will government-sponsored education and training facilities be adequately prepared to meet the volume and character of demand from these populations in the future?
3 What innovations in housing policy will be needed to meet the likely upsurge of demand in the "family forming" age groups?

Some of the most important issues connected with these populations are not raised, at least by implication, in the three questions just provided. This list is designed to highlight the issues that are closely connected with demographic trends, and is based upon an analysis of literature done by Hélène Gaudry Seni, in a special draft paper for this study.

In large urban centres, especially Toronto and Vancouver, ethnicity issues are becoming increasingly debated. As a result of changes in immigration regulations in the 1960s, the proportion of immigrants with ethnic origins other than those that have been traditionally dominant in Canada has risen significantly. The spectre of the radical alterations in Canadian culture as a result of this development is now continually raised in the popular press and is a subject of debate among concerned Canadians. The problem, and the potential for social unrest involved in these developments, is closely connected to the pattern of geographic concentration of the recent immigrants, and this is a major reason why the outcries are now coming mainly from Toronto and Vancouver. There is debate in these centres between those who see an intrinsic enrichment of Canadian life in the recent trends and those who see a deplorable threat to established local cultures.

With respect to the improvement of quality of life in Canadian cities, a number of substantial public policy issues are raised by the recent trends. First and foremost is the issue of determining the desirable ethnic or national origin composition of immigration to Canada. Secondly, there is a significant policy issue concerning the rate at which a number of important Canadian communities can reasonably be expected to absorb, without major disturbances, substantial concentrations of people from other countries. Policies to influence the geographic settlement pattern of immigrants to Canada may be relevant in this area.

Also relevant are policies that are concerned with the adjustment process within Canada not only of immigrants but also of the "receiving populations" in the pertinent Canadian communities. In this connection, policies that aim at gathering and disseminating more accurate information about the characteristics of immigrants and related adjustment problems in immigrant communities, and at facilitating the adjustment process, may be increasingly debated in this country.

3.4.5 Summary   Many individual attributes are involved in the subject of population composition. Future composition changes in Canada, and the unfolding lagged effects of past changes, are the sources of a great variety of social problems and public policy issues in Canada. The foregoing discussion in this section has merely touched briefly on a selection of issues, many of which are already being debated, but will continue to command attention. For the purposes of quick recollection some over-simplified titles may be cited to summarize the themes that were reviewed. In the field of education debate will continue on the issues related to productivity of the educational system; flexibility of human and non-human investments in the industry; militancy of teacher unions; expectations concerning the benefits of education; and optimal allocation of public tax revenues between educational and other purposes.

Only a few of the many important issues related to Canada's older population have been touched. These include determination of government responsibility in the provision of social services on behalf of the aged; co-ordination of the policies at different levels of government; adequacy of income; the age of retirement; inter-industry variation in pension benefits; equity in the extension of services to the aged; organization of work activity; recruitment practices of employers; education and retraining; health care; and housing.

The linguistic and ethnic compositions of the population are fertile areas for public policy issues in the late 1970s and the 1980s. Most important among such issues are those concerning the desirable linguistic balance and how it should be pursued. The growth and increasing educational attainment of the native Indian population will sharpen the issues of government responsibility to help promote employment and local economic development opportunities, adequate local education and training facilities, and innovations in housing policy. The desirable ethnic composition of immigration will continue to be debated, as will be the responsibility of government to enlighten the public about aspects of the immigrant adjustment process and to facilitate the process. The on-going debate about ways to influence the pattern of geographic concentration of immigrants will not be brought to a halt or rendered academic by future legislation.

4

GOVERNMENT POPULATION POLICIES[1]

4.1 Introduction

This chapter is a selective outline of government initiatives in the field of population policy. It can be said generally that few public policies have been adopted to reach demographic objectives. Those that seem closely related to demographic objectives, such as the Immigration Act, have in fact been adopted most often to meet a great number of needs which are quite different and sometimes contrary to the requirements of a certain control of demographic evolution. Although several pieces of legislation deal with demographic phenomena, the legislator has realized only recently the importance of the repercussions of demographic phenomena on most fields of activity in the management of community resources.

The purpose of this chapter is to selectively review government initiatives which would seem to be related to population trends. This review will consider not only the policies adopted to directly influence population trends, but also the initiatives which, while adopted for reasons other than their demographic impact, nevertheless take this impact into account. The demographic variables that will be considered are the following: the growth rate of the population, the components of that growth (mortality, fertility, nuptiality, and migration), the territorial population distribution, and, finally, some characteristics of population (age, sex, education, language, and ethnic origin).

4.2 Explicit Search for Population Policies

In recent years the federal government has actively taken up the possibility of greater co-ordination in the field of population policies. Since 1973, the Cabinet has reviewed a great number of pertinent documents from, among others, the Ministry of State for Urban Affairs, Manpower and Immigration, Regional Economic Expansion, and the Privy Council. These documents presented various alternatives that could eventually serve as bases for population policy.

The government studies led to the formation, in February 1975, of a Demographic Policy Steering Group. This Group is composed of deputy ministers, and is chaired by the representative of the co-ordinating

1. This chapter was originally written in French.

57

minister—the Minister of Manpower and Immigration. The Group is charged with developing a federal position on population policies, and with co-ordinating the federal input in related federal-provincial and public consultations. In consultation with provincial governments and the general public, the Steering Group plans to develop guidelines that may eventually encompass a network of interrelated policies which affect Canadian demographic trends. The fields touched by such policies would include regional development, urbanization, land use, transportation, communications, and industrial growth.

To help support the Steering Group, a National Demographic Policy Secretariat has been created to conduct consultations with the provinces and the general public. It will help to promote the co-ordination of federal-provincial activities related to demographic problems.

The province of Quebec has also undertaken a study on the population objectives it may wish to pursue (see Bonin, 1974). The first step in this study was the preparation of a document whose purpose is to identify the main components of the issue. The provincial Cabinet also requested the preparation of a white paper which was to state the main Quebec objectives in the field of population.

In the area of immigration, the federal government has undertaken a review of its policy. The Canadian government historically welcomed high immigration, which made possible such great development projects as the railroad and the opening of the West. During the second half of the nineteenth century, the Government of Canada took many initiatives to attract immigrants (advertising in northern European countries from 1856; subsidies to transport companies from 1872; land grants exemplified in the Free Grants and Homestead Act, 1868). The government also showed much concern about Canadian emigration to the United States. These efforts gave rise to an important flow of immigrants throughout the great Canadian economic expansion periods. Only in adverse economic periods, such as during the 1930s and both world wars, was the rate of flow substantially decreased.

While continuing to encourage immigration, the initiatives of the Canadian government during the 1960s have brought some control over the socio-economic composition of immigration. Regulations were introduced in 1962 with the intent to eliminate the discriminatory aspects of the Immigration Act and emphasize the levels of education and professional training of the immigrants. The establishment of the Department of Manpower and Immigration in 1966 confirmed the intended supportive role of immigration in the improvement of the quality of Canadian manpower.

Since the beginning of the 1970s there has been serious questioning of the importance of a high yearly volume of immigrants as a source of economic progress for Canada. This change of mind was brought about by three developments. First, the efforts in the field of education in

Canada during the 1950s and 1960s made less necessary an outside source of qualified labour force. Secondly, the anti-discriminatory rulings adopted in 1962 and maintained in 1966 have coincided with a gradual change in the distribution of immigrants by country of origin. Thirdly, there was the massive arrival on the labour market of the children born during the years of great fertility following the Second World War. Faced with continuing high unemployment rates, Canadians are showing increasing resistance to the idea of maintaining a high level of immigration.

Because of the impact of the developments just mentioned, the Minister of Manpower and Immigration testified that it was necessary "to try to undertake a much more profound examination and review of basic immigration policies within a framework of a comprehensive demographic approach, one that would inevitably involve a more prolonged effort engaging both the provincial governments, the federal government and the Canadian people on [sic] a hard look at long term goals and objectives. Formidable as it is, that is the choice that was made . . . " (Canada, Parliament, Special Joint Committee of the Senate and of the House of Commons on Immigration Policy, 9 April 1975a, p. 8).

When the Minister tabled the Green Paper on Immigration before Parliament (3 February 1975), he underlined once again that the orientation of immigration policies should rest on a national agreement on flexible guidelines with regard to demographic evolution in Canada. In the Minister's opinion, the new Act (on immigration) could well lead the government to regulate the immigration flow in terms of demographic policy objectives which will derive from necessarily dynamic and fluctuating conditions. Furthermore, the debate on the Canadian immigration policy should also take into account the latter's impact on regional expansion, urban growth, and land use policy. (See Canada, Parliament, Special Joint Committee of the Senate and of the House of Commons on Immigration Policy, 9 April 1975a, pp. 9-10.)

A joint committee of the House and Senate held nearly 50 public hearings on immigration policy in 21 cities during 1975. In the course of its work, the committee received more than 1,200 letters or briefs. Its final report was tabled later in 1975 (see Canada, Parliament, Special Joint Committee of the Senate and of the House of Commons on Immigration Policy, 1975b). Several aspects of immigration policy were dealt with in this report. Two recommendations that bear directly on demographic objectives may be mentioned in passing.

The joint committee concluded that Canada should continue to be a country of immigration. It recommended that "immigration in future be treated as a central variable in a national population policy and that this objective be achieved through the establishment of an immigration target to be adjusted from time to time to achieve an even rate of population growth as well as to take account of changing economic

59

conditions and needs." (Canada, Parliament, Special Joint Committee of the Senate and of the House of Commons on Immigration Policy, 1975b, p. 7.)

On the question of policy concerning the geographic distribution of future immigrants, the committee suggested means by which prospective immigrants might be encouraged to settle in specific parts of the country. Concerning the general objectives of such policy, the committee proposed that "area demand be . . . used experimentally to encourage prospective immigrants to settle in communities where population growth is desired and is compatible with regional development plans." (Canada, Parliament, Special Joint Committee of the Senate and of the House of Commons on Immigration Policy, 1975b, p. 29.)

4.3 Interventions by Governments

As we have just shown, governmental efforts are now being made to face demographic issues directly. Parallel with this relatively recent explicit search for population policy, the government has intervened and continues to intervene in the evolution of demographic phenomena in a variety of ways. The importance of the demographic ramifications of these interventions varies, as does the explicitness of concern with population objectives. The following sub-sections review aspects of these governmental interventions.

4.3.1 The population growth rate   As regards the desirable Canadian population growth rate over the next two decades, the Green Paper concluded in the following terms its review of the results of discussions provided by several government departments:

> Predictably an analysis of this exercise did not provide a firm basis for definite conclusions that one growth path was at all points necessarily to be preferred to the other. Nevertheless, it was not surprising that the survey brought out clearly that there were few areas of public policy where problems would be materially alleviated by a future spectrum of population growth in the higher of the two ranges. Accordingly, there was a general disposition to favour the more moderate upward curve. (Canada, Department of Manpower and Immigration, *Canadian Immigration and Population Study,* 1974a, 1:7.)

In practice, it thus seems that the federal government favours at least on the short-term a slowdown of growth. This orientation also emerges from recent decisions taken by the Minister of Manpower and Immigration whose purpose seems to be to appreciably reduce the number of immigrants per year. For example, on 22 February 1974, the

4.3.3 Language balance Until 1951 Canadian francophones managed to maintain their relative importance at about 30 percent of the Canadian population because of a higher than average rate of fertility, but the situation has changed significantly in recent years. If we add to this observation the importance of language transfers by persons of French mother tongue residing outside Quebec, and the general tendency for immigrants to choose English as their working language, it is easy to understand the increased interest among politicians towards the establishment of language objectives.

On 19 July 1963, the federal Cabinet established a Royal Commission on Bilingualism and Biculturalism in order to obtain an evaluation and recommendations concerning the situation of the two ethnic groups that originated the Canadian Confederation. When the Commission tabled its first report on bilingualism, it noted that "the importance of the linguistic question, often minimized in Canada, had to be emphasized" (Canada, Commission royale d'enquête sur le bilinguisme et le biculturalisme, *Rapport,* 1967, 1: xx).

The initiatives of the last decade at the federal level, which followed this comprehensive inquiry, are well-known. The principles of the language policy are stated both in the British North America Act and in the Official Languages Act enacted on 9 July 1969, which follows the recommendation of Book I of the Royal Commission on Bilingualism and Biculturalism. This Act provides the rationale for policies put forth by the federal government during the 1960s, particularly the policy on bilingualism in the public service (announced in the Commons by Prime Minister Lester Pearson on 6 April 1966). A language training program for public servants was launched in 1964.

The Official Languages Act also provided for the creation of regions where the government would undertake to give bilingual services. To reach that objective, the Act provides for the creation of an advisory board with members from the large regions of the country. The chairman was appointed on 12 February 1970. Originally, the board was to present its report, containing the list and boundaries of the bilingual districts, in fall 1973. Partly for reasons of availability of census data, the final report was tabled in December 1975.

The Quebec government is also very concerned with the evolution of the use of the French language. On 9 December 1968, it created by order-in-council the Commission of Inquiry on the Position of the French Language and on Language Rights in Quebec (usually called the Gendron Commission). This commission was to pursue the analysis of the linguistic issue, after the failure of a first legislation (Bill 63) on the status of the French language in Quebec. Following the work of the Gendron Commission, the Quebec government replaced Bill 63 with Bill 22, whose novel elements are the rules concerning the learning of French by immigrants who do not speak either of the two official languages on their arrival in Canada.

The preoccupation of the Quebec government with the language issue will remain important during the next few years, according to the authors of *Pour une problématique des ressources humaines au Québec.* This book anticipates that by the year 2000 between 92 percent and 93 percent of francophone Canadians will be living in Quebec. "But despite this concentration the French predominance in Quebec, demographically strong in most of Quebec, but much weaker in Montreal, seems threatened in the long-term; this proportion will probably reach between 77 to 79 percent around the year 2000" [2] (Bonin, 1974, p. 107).

Faced with this problematic situation, the authors offer the following commentary:

If we consider that these factors are important, it follows that first the Quebec population would do well to grow at the same rate as the rest of Canada. In this perspective, it would be advisable to give attention to migratory flows at least as much as to the birth rate. According to an evaluation by R. Maheu, Quebec could have lost a total of 24,000 people in international and interprovincial migrations from 1961 to 1971. As for the birth rate, some analysts believe they can state that it is not insufficient in itself when one disregards the temporary factors which made it fall below the level of the other Canadian provinces. However, if Quebec does not manage to enjoy a net immigration proportional to the rest of Canada (which has certainly been the case for the last few years), one could imagine balancing it by a surplus in the birth rate. . . . factors influencing the birth rate are so complex that such a result is far from being an established fact. As for the possibility of preventing the proportion of francophones in Quebec from falling, many types of actions can be taken: improve means of preventing francophones from leaving or see to it fewer emigrate in proportion to other Quebecers (Robert Maheu's estimates presented at a seminar for the Quebec Demographers' Association held at the University of Montreal on 24 November 1973 would show that the decade 1961–1971 was certainly not a success in that light); try to attract francophone immigrants, whether from other provinces or outside of Canada, and to francophonize non-francophone newcomers; try to increase the birth rate more among francophones than among non-francophones; or a combination of all these actions. For various reasons . . . on which J. Henripin has already begun an analysis, these possible actions all pose difficulties because of the size of the figures involved, and the cost of all of them is rather high. So even the implementation of this objective would be a difficult task.[3] (Bonin, 1974, pp. 109–10.)

2. Free translation.

3. Free translation.

4.3.4 Fertility, nuptiality, and mortality The federal government has maintained, until the recent decision to directly take up the issue of population growth, the position that fertility questions are personal and confidential and the state should not interfere.

In 1969, the government amended the Canada Criminal Code (section 237 (4)) to allow doctors to practice abortions once a committee on therapeutic abortions had stated in writing that without this abortion the life or health of the mother was in danger. The same year (18 August 1969), an amendment to section 150 (2) (c) of the Criminal Code abolished the legal obstacle (in application since 1892) to the advertising or selling of contraceptives.

On 18 September 1970, the Department of National Health and Welfare announced a research, training and information program in regard to family planning. Funds from subsidy programs of the Department of National Health and Welfare and the Medical Research Council (see Marsden, 1972, p. 42) were available to finance family planning clinics, to train personnel in these clinics, and to meet other expenses related to the spreading of information on family planning techniques.

In another field, labour, the government amended in 1971 the Unemployment Insurance Act so that the period of confinement and the one preceding and following it may be covered by unemployment insurance benefits. During the same period the government activated the issue of child care centres by facilitating the development of some of them through its Local Initiatives Program.

All these initiatives may have an impact on fertility. But it does not seem that this aspect of their possible effects was ever the determining factor in any of the policies. However, the federal government is considering sponsorship of a national inquiry on fertility. The Family Planning Division (Department of National Health and Welfare), in co-operation with Statistics Canada, is organizing the effort. At present the department has subsidized a group of demographers whose task will be to define the framework of the inquiry and to set the goals of such an inquiry.

With regard to nuptiality, Canadian governments, federal or provincial, do not seem interested in creating policies to guide the trend in the country's marriage or divorce rates. Certain government interventions have had effects on these two aspects of nuptiality. Only a few examples will be given here.

Canadian provincial governments have regulations concerning the minimum marriage age (with or without parents' consent). These rules partially determine the rate of marriages celebrated each year in the country. The Royal Commission on the Status of Women has made a recommendation concerning these regulations. As for divorce, the change in the policy adopted by the government in 1969 is well known. A new law allows a greater diversity of causes which can rightfully be invoked to obtain a divorce. The immediate effect of this change has been a major increase in requests for divorce in Canada since the adoption of this law in 1969.

Even though the mortality issue is not often raised in debates on population policies in Canada, certain policies result in lowering or eliminating any trend towards an increase in the mortality rate of the country. The efforts of the government seem firstly directed to the protection of the country's health; but the distance between health protection and lowering the mortality rate is small and easily crossed in most cases.

There are some cases in which it is obvious that the government policy is to try to directly lower the mortality rate. Examples include the efforts to lower the infant mortality rate; policies and regulations to reduce industrial and road accidents; and research grants to scientists studying degenerative diseases.

4.3.5 Manpower mobility The federal government has developed training programs for the unemployed, spread information on job opportunities, and subsidized moving expenses for certain categories of employees in search of work in the Maritimes.

As for training courses, the purpose of the government policy is to help some categories of workers to acquire new qualifications. Courses are given by the provinces and financed by the federal government. Regarding the diffusion of information on available jobs, the government has set up a network of manpower centres throughout Canada. For a detailed analysis of these government policies, reference should be made to the eighth annual review of the Economic Council of Canada (1971).

4.3.6 Education We do not intend to mention here all the different aspects of Canadian policies on education. Education is a field where governments have played a very active role particularly in the last 15 years. The only issue we will discuss in this volume concerns the population composition according to the level of education. The changes in this composition and rates of participation in different levels of school systems are very important aspects of the country's demographic trends. Aside from responding to the increased demand for education brought about by the baby boom cohort of the 1960s, Canadian governments have adopted policies aimed at significantly improving the quality of the educational attainment composition of the population. This is what the analyses of the Economic Council of Canada (1971), of Deutsch (1973), and of Harvey (1974) have clearly shown. Furthermore, there is now, in some provinces at least, a policy for the "democratization" of access to university training so that income and social status need no longer be determining factors.

4.4 Conclusion

In the next few years it seems that the essential content of demographic policies will be put into force through immigration policies and internal migration policies. In other words, it does not seem that the governments are very hopeful about their capacity to significantly influence mortality rates, fertility rates, and emigration from this country. The authors of the Green Paper deliver pertinent conclusions on this question:

> Even an abbreviated account of this sort is sufficient to indicate the difficulties involved in setting definite targets for overall rates of population expansion, the complexities surrounding judgments about the relative advantages of alternative rates, and the uncertainties involved in implementing policies to attain any given objective with respect to total numbers. There are few firm handholds for policy in the field of demographic planning. One, it has been emphasized, can be furnished through the control of immigration volume. (Canada, Department of Manpower and Immigration, *Canadian Immigration and Population Study*, 1974a, 1: 7.)

APPENDIX

Participants at the Montreal Seminars

In connection with this project, seminars were held on 15, 17, and 19 September 1975 at the Ritz Carlton Hotel in Montreal. The 42 participants were invited to give their views on (1) the issues of public policy that are likely to be of major importance during the next 10–15 years, with special attention to those related to population trends, and (2) research projects which may be helpful in dealing with those issues.

The participants represented a cross-section of Canadians with substantial experience and expertise in the areas of these themes. Their affiliations included the federal, provincial, and municipal governments, universities, crown corporations, and private research or social agencies. Their academic backgrounds covered such fields as demography, political science, sociology, anthropology, urban and regional planning, economics, and geography. Their professional interests included long-range planning, environmental studies, policy planning, policy research, manpower, immigration, finance, status of women, hospital planning, urban affairs, resource policy, education, land use, intergovernmental affairs, municipal affairs, and health and welfare. However, the participants were asked to speak in a personal capacity rather than as representatives of particular organizations. They were encouraged to speak in the official language in which they felt most comfortable since simultaneous translation services were available. A detailed list of participants, showing names and affiliations, is given at the end of this appendix.

Several background documents were circulated in advance to stimulate thought and discussion concerning the seminar topics. The first was a reference paper containing a collection of existing projections, a substantial portion of which forms chapter two of the present volume. In addition, nine participants were commissioned to prepare position papers to set the tone of each day's discussions. All participants received a set of the nine papers 10 to 15 days before the seminars. The authors had been asked to identify major policy issues that might be significantly related to designated areas of population change, and to state their views regarding the major and feasible research projects that ought to be pursued, either by IRPP or some other agency, in order to provide knowledge that they perceived to be badly needed by policy-makers and the public.

At each seminar, the three position paper authors were asked to give 20-minute summaries of their papers. Following these presentations the participants were invited to pick up the discussion and to bring in any other related questions or topics for a period of approximately one and a half hours. At the end of each day the chairman asked a few specific questions concerning the future work of the Institute, especially in connection with policy research related to population trends.

A list of authors and titles of position papers follows:

1. Jacques Henripin, "Population et politiques"
2. L. J. Byrne, "Potential Problems Associated with the Evolution of the Size and Composition of the Canadian Population in the 1980s"
3. Louis Parai, "Major Policy Issues and Research Projects Related to Canada's Demographic Size, Growth and Composition in the 1980s"
4. Lorna R. Marsden, "Ageing and the 1980s"
5. Frank T. Denton and Byron G. Spencer, "Towards a Program of Research on Population Change and its Economic Effects in the 1980s"
6. I. M. Timonin, "Socio-Economic Composition of the Canadian Population in the 1980s"
7. Gerald Hodge, "People, Place, and Policy"
8. H. N. Lash, "Policy Research on the Distribution of the Canadian Population"
9. H. L. Laframboise and John Chibuk, "Active Population Programs: A Research Perspective"

A complete list of the participants and their affiliations follows:

Mr. Ruben C. Bellan
Dean of Studies
St. John's College
University of Manitoba

Monsieur Georges Bonhomme
Surintendant
Division des Programmes
Service d'Urbanisme
Ville de Montréal

Monsieur Bernard Bonin
Sous-ministre adjoint
Ministère de l'Immigration
Gouvernement du Québec

Mr. L. J. Byrne
Director
Briefing Team
Privy Council Office
Government of Canada

Mr. George W. Cadbury
Chairman of Governing Body
International Planned Parenthood
    Federation

Mr. John A. Clark
Director of Hospital Planning
Capital Regional Hospital District
Victoria, British Columbia

Mr. George Courage
Director of Central Statistical
    Services
Economic and Resource Policy
Office of the Executive Council
Government of Newfoundland

Professor Frank T. Denton
Department of Economics
McMaster University

Mr. David A. Dodge
Executive Director
Market and Industry Analysis Division
Central Mortgage and Housing Corporation
Government of Canada

Professor Lorne W. Downey
Centre for the Study of
    Administration in Education
Faculty of Education
University of British Columbia

Mrs. M. I. Eady
Director
Women's Bureau
Department of Labour
Government of Manitoba

Professor Leonard Gertler
School of Urban and Regional
    Planning
Faculty of Environmental Studies
University of Waterloo

Mr. Ted Harvey
Director
Research Group
Social Planning Council of
    Metropolitan Toronto

Mr. Jim Hayes
Director
Planning and Systems
Department of the Secretary
    of State
Government of Canada

Professeur Jacques Henripin
Département de Démographie
Université de Montréal

Professor Gerald Hodge
School of Urban and Regional
    Planning
Queen's University

Mr. Frank J. Kelly
Science Adviser
Science Council of Canada

Professor Leszek Kosinski
Department of Geography
University of Alberta

Mr. H. L. Laframboise
Assistant Secretary
Policy and Research Wing
Urban Growth and Land
Ministry of State for Urban Affairs
Government of Canada

Mr. Bill Lampert
Economist
Policy Planning Branch
Ministry of Treasury, Economics and
    Intergovernmental Affairs
Government of Ontario

Monsieur Pierre E. Laporte
Directeur de la recherche
    socio-économique
Régie de la langue française
Gouvernement du Québec

Mr. H. N. Lash
Former Chairman
Greater Vancouver Regional District

Professeur Jacques Légaré
Département de Démographie
Université de Montréal

Professor N. Harvey Lithwick
Department of Economics
Carleton University

Professor Betty Macleod
Department of Educational Planning
The Ontario Institute for Studies
    in Education

Mr. Frank Marlyn
Director
Special Projects and Policy
    Research Branch
Department of Municipal Affairs
Government of Alberta

Professor Lorna R. Marsden
Department of Sociology
University of Toronto

Mr. Glen G. D. Milne
Consultant
Priorities and Planning Secretariat
Privy Council Office
Government of Canada

Monsieur Edmund M. Murphy
Directeur de la recherche "A"
Groupe des Travaux de Recherche
Division de la recherche et de la
  planification stratégique
Ministère de la Main-d'oeuvre
  et de l'Immigration
Gouvernement du Canada

Mr. Louis Parai
Chief
General Economic Conditions Section
Economic Analysis Division
Department of Finance
Government of Canada

Mr. W. D. Parasiuk
Secretary
Planning Secretariat of Cabinet
Government of Manitoba

Monsieur André Raynauld
Président
Conseil Économique du Canada

Professor Anthony H. Richmond
Department of Sociology
York University

Mr. Saul N. Silverman
Consulting Political Scientist

Professor Byron G. Spencer
Department of Economics
McMaster University

Mr. Chris Taylor
Department of Geography
University of Toronto

Mr. Ivan Timonin
Director
National Demographic Policy
  Secretariat
Department of Manpower and
  Immigration
Government of Canada

Professor Frank G. Vallee
Department of Sociology
Carleton University

Mr. E. J. van Goudoever
Director
Long Range Planning (Welfare)
Department of National Health
  and Welfare
Government of Canada

Mr. Michael Wolfson
Policy Analyst
Planning Branch
Effectiveness Division
Treasury Board
Government of Canada

Dr. John Young
Assistant Deputy Minister
Economic Programs and Government
  Finance Branch
Department of Finance
Government of Canada

Dr. E. Ziegler
Director
Urban Program Evaluation Group
Ministry of State for Urban Affairs
Government of Canada

REFERENCES

Bogue, Donald. *Principles of Demography.* New York: Wiley, 1969.

Bonin, Bernard, éd. *Une problématique des ressources humaines au Québec.* Montréal: Ministère de l'Immigration, 1974.

Canada. Bilingual Districts Advisory Board. *Report of the Bilingual Districts Advisory Board.* Ottawa: Information Canada, 1975.

Canada. Commission royale d'enquête sur le bilinguisme et le biculturalisme. *Rapport.* Ottawa: Imprimeur de la Reine, 1967.

Canada. Department of Manpower and Immigration. *Report of the Canadian Immigration and Population Study.* Vol. 1: *Immigration Policy Perspectives.* Ottawa: Information Canada, 1974a.

Canada. Dominion Bureau of Statistics. *1951 Census of Canada.* Vol. 2: *Population—Cross Classification of Characteristics.* Ottawa: Queen's Printer.

Canada. Dominion Bureau of Statistics. *1961 Census of Canada.* Vol. 1 (Part 3): *Population.* Cat. No. 92-552 — 92-564. Ottawa: Queen's Printer.

Canada. Ministry of State for Urban Affairs. Demographic Research Group. Policy and Research Wing. "Interim Population Projections of 22 Census Metropolitan Areas, 1971-2001." Discussion paper B75.10. Ottawa: Ministry of State for Urban Affairs, 1975b.

Canada. Parlement. Chambre des communes. Comité permanent de la santé, du bien-être social et des affaires sociales. *Procès-verbaux et témoignages concernant: Budget principal 1974-1975, Département d'État chargé des Affaires urbaines.* N° 1, 15 octobre 1974. Ottawa: Information Canada, 1974b.

Canada. Parliament. House of Commons. Standing Committee on Labour, Manpower and Immigration. *Minutes of Proceedings, 1975-.* Ottawa: Information Canada, 1975.

Canada. Parliament. Special Joint Committee of the Senate and of the House of Commons on Immigration Policy. *Minutes of Proceedings, 1975-.* Ottawa: Information Canada, 1975a.

Canada. Parliament. Special Joint Committee of the Senate and of the House of Commons on Immigration Policy. *Report to Parliament: Immigration.* Ottawa: Information Canada, 1975b.

REFERENCES

Canada. Statistics Canada. *1971 Census of Canada.* Vol. 1 (Part 1): *Population—Census Subdivisions (Historical).* Cat. No. 92-702. Ottawa: Information Canada, 1973.

Canada. Statistics Canada. *1971 Census of Canada.* Vol. 1 (Part 1): *Population—Urban and Rural Distributions.* Cat. No. 92-709. Ottawa: Information Canada, 1973.

Canada. Statistics Canada. *1971 Census of Canada.* Vol. 1 (Part 3): *Population—Ethnic Groups.* Cat. No. 92-723. Ottawa: Information Canada, 1973.

Canada. Statistics Canada. *1971 Census of Canada.* Vol. 1 (Part 3): *Population—Mother Tongue.* Cat. No. 92-725. Ottawa: Information Canada, 1974.

Canada. Statistics Canada. *1971 Census of Canada.* Vol. 1 (Part 4): *Population—Language by Ethnic Groups.* Cat. No. 92-736. Ottawa: Information Canada, 1974.

Canada. Statistics Canada. *1971 Census of Canada.* Vol. 2 (Part 1): *Households—Households by Size.* Cat. No. 93-702. Ottawa: Information Canada, 1973.

Canada. Statistics Canada. *1971 Census of Canada.* Vol. 2 (Part 2): *Families—Families by Size and Type.* Cat. No. 93-714. Ottawa: Information Canada, 1973.

Canada. Statistics Canada. *Population Projections for Canada and the Provinces, 1972-2001.* Cat. No. 91-514. Ottawa: Information Canada, 1974.

Canada. Task Force on Housing and Urban Development. *Report.* Ottawa: Queen's Printer, 1969.

Deutsch, John. "The University Today and Tomorrow." *CAUT Bulletin* 21 (June 1973): 4-9.

Economic Council of Canada. *Fourth Annual Review: The Canadian Economy from the 1960's to the 1970's.* Ottawa: Queen's Printer, 1967.

Economic Council of Canada. *Eighth Annual Review: Design for Decision-Making—An Application to Human Resources Policies.* Ottawa: Information Canada, 1971.

Economic Council of Canada. "Immigration and National Policy." A presentation to the Special Joint Committee of the Senate and of the House of Commons on Immigration Policy, Ottawa, 8 May 1975a.

Economic Council of Canada. *Twelfth Annual Review: Options for Growth.* Ottawa: Information Canada, 1975b.

Harvey, Edward. *Educational Systems and the Labour Market.* Don Mills: Longman, 1974.

Henripin, Jacques. *Immigration and Language Imbalance.* Study commissioned for the Canadian Immigration and Population Study. Ottawa: Information Canada, 1974.

Joy, Richard. *Languages in Conflict: The Canadian Experience.* Ottawa: The Author, 1967.

Kirkland, John S. *Demographic Aspects of Housing Demand to 1986.* Ottawa: Central Mortgage and Housing Corporation, 1971.

Lithwick, N.H. *Urban Canada: Problems and Prospects.* Ottawa: Central Mortgage and Housing Corporation, 1970.

Maheu, Robert. *Les francophones du Canada, 1941-1991.* Montréal: Éditions Parti pris, 1970.

Marsden, Lorna R. *Population Probe.* Toronto: Copp Clark, 1972.

Municipality of Metropolitan Toronto. *Choices for the Future. Summary Report: Metropolitan Toronto Transportation Plan Review.* Toronto: Ministry of Transportation and Communications, 1975.

Organisation for Economic Co-operation and Development. *Demographic Trends 1970–1985 in OECD Member Countries.* Paris: OECD, 1974.

Québec. Ministère des Affaires municipales. *L'urbanisation au Québec: Rapport du groupe de travail sur l'urbanisation* (Rapport Castonguay). Québec: Éditeur officiel du Québec, 1976.

Reynolds, D.J. *Urban Transport Problem.* Research Monograph no. 3. Ottawa: Central Mortgage and Housing Corporation, 1971.

Science Council of Canada. "Population and Technology." Paper no. 7. A draft report prepared by the Committee on Population and Technology. Ottawa: Science Council of Canada, 1975.

Stone, Leroy O. *Urban Development in Canada.* 1961 Census Monograph. Ottawa: Queen's Printer, 1967.

United Nations. Department of Economic and Social Affairs. *World Population Prospects as Assessed in 1963.* Population Studies, no. 41. New York: United Nations, 1966.

Zsigmond, Zoltan E., and Rechnitzer, Edith. *Projected Potential Labour Force Entrants from the Canadian Educational Systems, 1971 to 1985.* Ottawa: Statistics Canada, 1974.

SELECTED BIBLIOGRAPHY

In the following bibliography the citations are classified under a series of subject headings, in order to assist the reader to probe more deeply into matters raised in the text. Separate alphabetical order of items by author is maintained *within* each subject heading. The headings are as follows:

Education
Energy, Resources, Technology
Fertility and Nuptiality
Growth of National Population
Immigration and Internal Migration
Language and Ethnic Origin
Manpower
Mortality and Morbidity
Older Population of Canada
Regional Development
Social Welfare and Social Services
Urban and Metropolitan Affairs
Miscellaneous

Education

Baker, Harold S. *The Future and Education, Alberta 1970–2005.* Edmonton: Human Resources Research Council of Alberta, 1971.

Canada. Statistics Canada. *Advance Statistics of Education, 1974–75.* Cat. No. 81–220. Ottawa: Information Canada, 1974.

Committee of Presidents of Universities of Ontario. *Towards 2000, the Future of Post-Secondary Education in Ontario.* A brief prepared for the Ontario Commission on Post-Secondary Education. Toronto: McClelland & Stewart, 1971.

Deutsch, John. "The University Today and Tomorrow." *CAUT Bulletin* 21 (June 1973): 4–9.

Harvey, Edward. *Educational Systems and the Labour Market.* Don Mills: Longman, 1974.

Holland, J., Quazi, S., Siddiqui, F., and Skolnik, M. *Manpower Forecasting and Educational Policy.* Study prepared for the Ontario Commission on Post-Secondary Education. Toronto: Queen's Printer, 1972.

Katz, Joseph. *Education in Canada.* World Education Series. Vancouver: Douglas, David & Charles, 1974.

Macleod, Betty, ed. *Demography and Educational Planning.* Monograph Series no. 7. Toronto: Ontario Institute for Studies in Education, 1970.

Ontario. Commission on Post-Secondary Education in Ontario. *Post-Secondary Education in Ontario: a Statement of Issues.* Toronto: Queen's Printer, 1969.

Porter, John. "Post-Industrialism, Post-Nationalism and Post-Secondary Education." *Canadian Public Administration* 14, no. 1 (Spring 1971): 32–50.

Wisenthal, M., Rechnitzer, E., and Zsigmond, Z. "Educational Attainment of Canadians: Looking Ahead." *The Canadian Business Review* 1, no. 2 (Spring 1974): 20–23.

Zsigmond, Z.E., and Wenaas, C.J. *Enrolment in Educational Institutions by Province, 1951–52 to 1980–81.* Economic Council of Canada, Staff Study no. 25. Ottawa: Queen's Printer, 1970.

Zsigmond, Zoltan. "Impact of Projected Population Trends on Post-Secondary Education 1961–2001." Paper presented to the Statistical Science Association of Canada at the annual meeting of the Learned Societies, Edmonton, 30 May 1975.

Zsigmond, Zoltan. "Toward 2001 A.D." Ottawa: Statistics Canada, Education, Science and Culture Division, 1975.

Energy, Resources, Technology

Carr, A. Barry, and Culver, David W. "Agriculture, Population and the Environment." Commission on Population Growth and the American Future. Research Reports, Vol. 3. *Population, Resources and the Environment,* edited by Ronald G. Ridker, pp. 181-211. Washington, D.C.: Government Printing Office, 1972.

Conseil des sciences du Canada. *Les options énergétiques du Canada.* Conseil des sciences du Canada, rapport n° 23. Ottawa: Information Canada, 1975.

Darmstadter, Joel. "Energy." Commission on Population Growth and the American Future. Research Reports, Vol. 3. *Population, Resources and the Environment,* edited by Ronald G. Ridker, pp. 103-49. Washington, D.C.: Government Printing Office, 1972.

Ontario. Advisory Committee on Energy. *Energy in Ontario, the Outlook and Policy Implications.* 2 vols. Toronto: Queen's Printer, 1972-1973.

Ontario. Task Force on the Human Environment. *Toward an Environmental Action Plan, in Response to the Conference on the Human Environment, Stockholm, June 1972.* Toronto: Queen's Printer, 1974.

Ridker, Ronald G. "Resource and Environmental Consequences of Population Growth in the United States: A Summary." Commission on Population Growth and the American Future. Research Reports, Vol. 3. *Population, Resources and the Environment,* edited by Ronald G. Ridker, pp. 17-33. Washington, D.C.: Government Printing Office, 1972.

Science Council of Canada. "Population and Technology." Paper no. 7. A draft report prepared by the Committee on Population and Technology. Ottawa: Science Council of Canada, 1975.

Sewell, W.R. Derrick, and Bower, Blair T. *Forecasting the Demands for Water.* Ottawa: Queen's Printer, 1968.

Fertility and Nuptiality

Canada. Department of National Health and Welfare. *Current Status of Family Planning in Canada.* Ottawa: Department of National Health and Welfare, 1971.

Canada. Parliament. Special Joint Committee of the Senate and of the House of Commons on Divorce. *Report.* Ottawa: Queen's Printer, 1967.

Hepworth, H. Philip. *Personal Social Services in Canada: A Review.* Vol. 5. *Family Planning and Abortion Services and Family Life Education Programs.* Ottawa: Canadian Council on Social Development, 1975a.

Hersch, L. "The Fall of the Birth Rate and Its Effects on Social Policy." *International Labour Review* 28, no. 2 (August 1933): 153-67.

Growth of National Population

Barber, C.L. "Some Implications of the Move Towards Zero Population Growth in Developed Countries Upon the Level of Capital Expenditures." Discussion Paper, no. 19. Ottawa: Economic Council of Canada, 1975.

Basford, Ron. "La gestion de la croissance." Discours du Ministre d'État aux Affaires urbaines à la deuxième conférence tripartite, Edmonton, 22 octobre 1973c.

SELECTED BIBLIOGRAPHY

Calgary, Alta. Planning Department. *Metropolitan Calgary Population Projections, 1970-1991.* Calgary: City of Calgary Planning Department, 1970.

Canada. Dominion Bureau of Statistics. *1961 Census of Canada.* Vol. 1 (Part 3): *Population.* Cat. No. 92-552 — 92-564. Ottawa: Queen's Printer.

Canada. Statistics Canada. *Population Projections for Canada and the Provinces, 1972-2001.* Cat. No. 91-514. Ottawa: Information Canada, 1974.

Canada. Statistics Canada. *Technical Report on Population Projections for Canada and the Provinces, 1972-2001.* Cat. No. 91-516. Ottawa: Information Canada, 1975.

Conservation Foundation. "As Concern Over the Population Problem Mounts, the Nation Searches for a Policy." *Conservation Foundation Letter* (July 1970), pp. 1-16.

Corbet, P.S., and Smith, S.M. "A Population Policy for Canada." In *A Population Policy for Canada?* Proceedings of 2 seminars: "The Need for a Canadian Population Policy," held at the Ontario Institute for Studies in Education, Toronto, 20-21 November 1972, and "The Impact of People on the Environment," held at United Church House, Toronto, 10-11 May 1973. Toronto: Family Planning Federation of Canada, 1973.

Corbet, Philip S., and Le Roux, E.J. "The Population Problem: A Vital Canadian Policy Issue." *Science Forum* 5, no. 1 (February 1972): 25.

Illing, Wolfgang M. *Population, Family, Household and Labour Force Growth to 1980.* Economic Council of Canada, Staff Study no. 19. Ottawa: Queen's Printer, 1967.

Illing, Wolfgang M. "Population, Households, and Labour Supply to 1980." *Canada Manpower Review* 6, no. 1 (1973): 11-19.

Lachapelle, Réjean. "Evaluation of Population Projections Published by Statistics Canada." An appendix to "Illustrative Projections for the Population of Canada 1971-1991: Compilation and Adjustment of Existing Data," edited by Leroy O. Stone. Paper prepared for the Institute for Research on Public Policy. Montreal 1975a.

Marson, W.K., and Brown, G.E. "Considerations of a Population Policy for Canada." In *A Population Policy for Canada?* Proceedings of 2 seminars: "The Need for a Canadian Population Policy," held at the Ontario Institute for Studies in Education, Toronto, 20-21 November 1972, and "The Impact of People on the Environment," held at United Church House, Toronto, 10-11 May 1973. Toronto: Family Planning Federation of Canada, 1973.

Organisation for Economic Co-operation and Development. *Demographic Trends 1970-1985 in OECD Member Countries.* Paris: OECD, 1974.

Systems Research Group. *Canada: Population Projections to the Year 2000.* Toronto: Systems Research Group, 1970b.

Taylor, C.E. "Population and Growth." In *A Population Policy for Canada?* Proceedings of 2 seminars: "The Need for a Canadian Population Policy," held at the Ontario Institute for Studies in Education, Toronto, 20–21 November 1972, and "The Impact of People on the Environment," held at United Church House, Toronto, 10–11 May 1973. Toronto: Family Planning Federation of Canada, 1973.

Timlin, Mabel. *Does Canada Need More People?* Toronto: Oxford University Press, 1951.

United Nations. Department of Economic and Social Affairs. *World Population Prospects as Assessed in 1963.* Population Studies, no. 41. New York: United Nations, 1966.

U.S. Commission on Population Growth and the American Future. *Population and the American Future: Final Report.* Washington, D.C.: Government Printing Office, 1972.

Immigration and Internal Migration

Andras, Robert. Notes for an address by the Minister of Manpower and Immigration to the Atlantic Provinces Economic Council, Halifax, 27 June 1975a.

Andras, Robert. Notes for an address by the Minister of Manpower and Immigration to the Joint Meeting of the American Society of Planning Officials and the Community Planning Association of Canada, Vancouver, 13 April 1975b.

Andras, Robert. Statement by the Minister of Manpower and Immigration on Tabling of the Green Paper on Immigration Policy in the House of Commons, 3 February 1975c.

L'Association des démographes du Québec. "Pour donner chance égale à tous les candidats, il faudrait choisir au hasard les futurs immigrants." *Le Devoir,* 2 juillet 1975.

Badenduck, Tore. "Canadian Immigration and Population Policy." A paper submitted to the Special Joint Committee of the Senate and of the House of Commons on Immigration Policy, Toronto, June 1975.

SELECTED BIBLIOGRAPHY

Breton, Raymond, Armstrong, Jill, and Kennedy, Les. *The Social Impact of Changes in Population Size and Composition — Reactions to Patterns of Immigration.* Study commissioned for the Canadian Immigration and Population Study. Ottawa: Information Canada, 1974.

Canada. Department of Manpower and Immigration. *Internal Migration and Immigrant Settlement.* Ottawa: Information Canada, 1975.

Canada. Department of Manpower and Immigration. *Report of the Canadian Immigration and Population Study.* Vol. 1: *Immigration Policy Perspectives.* Ottawa: Information Canada, 1974a.

Canada. Department of Manpower and Immigration. *Report of the Canadian Immigration and Population Study.* Vol. 2: *The Immigration Program.* Ottawa: Information Canada, 1974b.

Canada. Department of Manpower and Immigration. *Report of the Canadian Immigration and Population Study.* Vol. 3: *Immigration and Population Statistics.* Ottawa: Information Canada, 1974c.

Canada. Department of Manpower and Immigration. *Report of the Canadian Immigration and Population Study.* Vol. 4: *Three Years in Canada.* Ottawa: Information Canada, 1974d.

Canada. Department of Manpower and Immigration. Canadian Immigration and Population Study. *Highlights from the Green Paper on Immigration and Population.* Ottawa: Information Canada, 1975.

Canada. Ministère de la Main-d'oeuvre et de l'Immigration. *La politique d'immigration du Canada.* Ottawa: Imprimeur de la Reine, 1966.

Canada. Parliament. Special Joint Committee of the Senate and of the House of Commons on Immigration Policy. *Minutes of Proceedings, 1975-.* Ottawa: Information Canada, 1975a.

Canada. Parliament. Special Joint Committee of the Senate and of the House of Commons on Immigration Policy. *Report to Parliament: Immigration.* Ottawa: Information Canada, 1975b.

Canadian Population Society. "Brief Concerning the Green Paper on Immigration." *Canadian Population Society Newsletter* 1, no. 1 (1975): 8–14.

Economic Council of Canada. "Immigration and National Policy." A presentation to the Special Joint Committee of the Senate and of the House of Commons on Immigration Policy, Ottawa, 8 May 1975a.

Epstein, Larry. *Immigration and Inflation.* Study commissioned for the Canadian Immigration and Population Study. Ottawa: Information Canada, 1974.

Hawkins, Freda. *Canada and Immigration: Public Policy and Public Concern.* Montreal: McGill-Queen's University Press, 1972.

Hawkins, Freda. "Immigration and Cities: a Report on the Green Paper on Immigration Policy." *Urban Forum* 1, no. 1 (Spring 1975): 7–13.

Hawkins, Freda. *Immigration Policy and Management in Selected Countries.* Study commissioned for the Canadian Immigration and Population Study. Ottawa: Information Canada, 1974.

Jackson, James M. "Canada and the Brain Drain." Master's Thesis, University of Western Ontario, 1974.

Kalbach, W.E. "Demographic Concerns and the Control of Immigration." *Canadian Public Policy* 1, no. 3 (Summer 1975): 302–10.

Kalbach, Warren E. *The Effect of Immigration on Population.* Study commissioned for the Canadian Immigration and Population Study. Ottawa: Information Canada, 1974.

Marr, William. "Labour Market and Other Implications of Immigration Policy." A research proposal. Kitchener: Wilfrid Laurier University, 1975.

Ontario Economic Council. *Immigrant Integration.* Toronto: Ontario Economic Council, 1970.

Parai, Louis. *The Economic Impact of Immigration.* Study commissioned for the Canadian Immigration and Population Study. Ottawa: Information Canada, 1974.

Québec. Ministère de l'Immigration. "La position du gouvernement du Québec à la suite de la publication du livre vert fédéral sur la politique canadienne d'immigration." Québec: Ministère de l'Immigration, avril 1975.

Richmond, Anthony H. *Aspects of the Absorption and Adaptation of Immigrants.* Study commissioned for the Canadian Immigration and Population Study. Ottawa: Information Canada, 1974.

Star, S. "In Search of a Rational Immigration Policy." *Canadian Public Policy* 1, no. 3 (Summer 1975): 328–42.

Tienhaara, Nancy. *Canadian Views on Immigration and Population — An Analysis of Post-War Gallup Polls.* Study commissioned for the Canadian Immigration and Population Study. Ottawa: Information Canada, 1974.

Language and Ethnic Origin

Canada. Bilingual Districts Advisory Board. *Report of the Bilingual Districts Advisory Board.* Ottawa: Information Canada, 1975.

Canada. Commission royale d'enquête sur le bilinguisme et le biculturalisme. *Rapport.* Ottawa: Imprimeur de la Reine, 1967.

Canada. Dominion Bureau of Statistics. *1951 Census of Canada.* Vol. 2: *Population — Cross Classification of Characteristics.* Ottawa: Queen's Printer.

Canada. Statistics Canada. *1971 Census of Canada.* Vol. 1 (Part 3): *Population — Ethnic Groups.* Cat. No. 92–723. Ottawa: Information Canada, 1973.

Canada. Statistics Canada. *1971 Census of Canada.* Vol. 1 (Part 3): *Population — Mother Tongue.* Cat. No. 92–725. Ottawa: Information Canada, 1974.

Canada. Statistics Canada. *1971 Census of Canada.* Vol. 1 (Part 4): *Population — Language by Ethnic Groups.* Cat. No. 92–736. Ottawa: Information Canada, 1974.

Cardinal, Harold. *The Unjust Society: The Tragedy of Canada's Indians.* Edmonton: Hurtig, 1969.

Charbonneau, Hubert, et Maheu, Robert. *Les aspects démographiques de la question linguistique.* Québec: Éditeur officiel du Québec, 1973.

Coulombe, Pierre. "Les langues officielles dans la fonction publique." Ottawa: Conseil du Trésor, 1972.

Didier, René. *Le processus des choix linguistiques des immigrants au Québec.* Québec: Éditeur officiel du Québec, 1973.

Frideres, J.S. *Canada's Indians: Contemporary Conflicts.* Scarborough, Ontario: Prentice-Hall, 1974.

Henripin, Jacques. *Immigration and Language Imbalance.* Study commissioned for the Canadian Immigration and Population Study. Ottawa: Information Canada, 1974.

Innis, Hugh R. *Bilingualism and Biculturalism: An Abridged Version of the Royal Commission Report.* Toronto: McClelland & Stewart, in co-operation with the Department of the Secretary of State and Information Canada, 1973.

Joy, Richard. *Languages in Conflict: The Canadian Experience.* Ottawa: The Author, 1967.

Maheu, Robert. "L'avenir des groupes linguistiques au Québec: l'aspect démographique." *Bulletin de l'Association des démographes du Québec* 2, spécial n° 2 (novembre 1973): 4-24.

Maheu, Robert. *Les francophones du Canada, 1941-1991.* Montréal: Éditions Parti pris, 1970.

Quebec. Commission of Inquiry on the Position of the French Language and on Language Rights in Quebec. *Report.* Vol. 1: *Language of Work.* Quebec: Éditeur officiel du Québec, 1972a.

Quebec. Commission of Inquiry on the Position of the French Language and on Language Rights in Quebec. *Report.* Vol. 2: *Language Rights.* Quebec: Éditeur officiel du Québec, 1972b.

Quebec. Commission of Inquiry on the position of the French Language and on Language Rights in Quebec. *Report.* Vol. 3: *The Ethnic Groups.* Quebec: Éditeur officiel du Québec, 1972c.

Manpower

Ahamad, B. *Projections of Manpower Requirements by Occupation in 1975: Canada and Its Regions.* Ottawa: Queen's Printer, 1969.

Bonin, Bernard, éd. *Une problématique des ressources humaines au Québec.* Montréal: Ministère de l'Immigration, 1974.

Canada. Parliament. House of Commons. Standing Committee on Labour, Manpower and Immigration. *Minutes of Proceedings, 1975-.* Ottawa: Information Canada, 1975.

Canada. Parliament. Senate. Special Committee on Manpower and Immigration. *Minutes of Proceedings, 1960-61.* Ottawa: Queen's Printer, 1960-1961.

Canada. Statistics Canada. *Historical Labour Force Statistics, Actual Data, Seasonal Factors, Seasonally Adjusted Data, 1973.* Cat. No. 71-201. Ottawa: Information Canada, 1974.

Economic Council of Canada. *Twelfth Annual Review: Options for Growth.* Ottawa: Information Canada, 1975b.

Organisation for Economic Co-operation and Development. *Manpower Policy and Programmes in Canada.* Paris: OECD, 1966.

Ostry, Sylvia, and Zaidi, Mahmood A. *Labour Economics in Canada.* Toronto: Macmillan, 1972.

Spengler, Joseph J. "Some Effects of Changes in the Age Composition of the Labor Force." *Southern Economic Journal* 8, no. 2 (1941): 157-75.

U.S. Department of Labor. Bureau of Labor Statistics. *The U.S. Economy in 1980; a Summary of BLS Projections.* Bulletin 1673 (1970).

Ziegler, E. "Manpower Challenges of the 1970's." *Canada Manpower Review 5, no.2 (1972): 1-8.*

Zsigmond, Zoltan E., and Rechnitzer, Edith. *Projected Potential Labour Force Entrants from the Canadian Educational Systems, 1971 to 1985.* Ottawa: Statistics Canada, 1974.

Mortality and Morbidity

Andersen, R., and Hull, J.T. "Hospital Utilization and Cost Trends in Canada and the United States." *Medical Care* 7 (November—December 1969): 4-22.

SELECTED BIBLIOGRAPHY

Anderson, O.W. "The Utilization of Health Services." In *Handbook of Medical Sociology,* edited by H. Freeman et al. Englewood Cliffs, N.J.: Prentice-Hall, 1963.

Anderson, O.W., and Andersen, R. "Patterns of Use of Health Services." In *Handbook of Medical Sociology,* 2nd ed., edited by H. Freeman et al. Englewood Cliffs, N.J.: Prentice-Hall, 1972.

Bayne, J.R.D. "Implications of Changing Age Structure of the Canadian Population, Community Health Services: Present and Future." Paper presented at the Science Council Committee on Population and Technology, Working Party on the Implications of a Changing Age Structure, Ottawa, January 1975.

Boudreau, Thomas J. *L'économique de la santé.* Sherbrooke: Université de Sherbrooke, 1967.

Canada. Department of National Health and Welfare. *Health Services in Canada 1973.* Ottawa: Department of National Health and Welfare, 1973a.

Canada. Department of National Health and Welfare. *A New Perspective on the Health of Canadians: A Working Document.* Ottawa: Department of National Health and Welfare, 1974a.

Canada. Department of National Health and Welfare. *Nutrition: A National Priority. A Report by Nutrition Canada.* Ottawa: Information Canada, 1973b.

Canada. Parlement. Chambre des communes. Comité permanent de la santé, du bien-être social et des affaires sociales. *Procès-verbaux et témoignages concernant: Budget principal 1975–1976, Conseil de recherches médicales.* N° 23, 29 mai 1975. Ottawa: Information Canada, 1975b.

Canada. Parlement. Chambre des communes. Comité permanent de la santé, du bien-être social et des affaires sociales. *Procès-verbaux et témoignages concernant: Budget principal 1975–1976, Santé nationale et bien-être social.* N° 12, 15 avril 1975. Ottawa: Information Canada, 1975c.

Canada. Royal Commission on Health Services. *Report.* 2 vols. Ottawa: Queen's Printer, 1964–1965.

Canada. Royal Commission on Health Services. *Studies.* 14 vols. Ottawa: Queen's Printer, 1965–1966.

Canada. Task Force on the Cost of Health Services in Canada. *Reports.* 3 vols. Ottawa: Queen's Printer, 1970.

Hanson, Eric J. *Public Finance Aspects of Health Services in Canada.* Study prepared for the Royal Commission on Health Services. Ottawa: Queen's Printer, 1964.

Québec. Commission d'enquête sur la santé et le bien-être social. *Rapport.* 7 vol. Québec: Éditeur officiel du Québec, 1969-1971.

Québec. Office de planification et de développement. *Mission de planification régionale Saguenay-Lac St-Jean: Esquisse du plan de développement.* Vol. 12: *Santé.* Québec: Éditeur officiel du Québec. 1969-.

Robertson, H. Rocke. *Health Care in Canada: A Commentary.* Science Council of Canada, Special Study, no. 29. Ottawa: Information Canada, 1973.

Stewart, Charles T. "Allocation of Resources to Health." *Journal of Human Resources* 6, no. 1 (Winter 1971): 103-22.

Older Population of Canada

Bairstow, Dale. "Demographic and Economic Aspects of Housing Canada's Elderly." Ottawa: Central Mortgage and Housing Corporation, 1973.

Baum, Daniel J. *The Final Plateau: The Betrayal of Our Older Citizens.* Toronto: Burns and MacEachern, 1974.

Bayne, J. R. D., ed. "Aging and Health." Background paper prepared for the Canadian Conference on Aging, 1966. Ottawa: Canadian Welfare Council, 1966.

Beattie, Walter M., Jr. "Aging and the Social Services." In *Handbook on the Social Sciences and Aging,* edited by R. H. Binstock and E. Shanas. New York: Van Nostrand Reinhold, forthcoming.

Birch, Norman E., and Koroluk, Susan H. *Study of the Continuum of Care for Senior Adults in Alberta.* Edmonton: Alberta Council on Aging, 1974.

Bortz, Edward L. "Our Aging Population: What it Means to You and All Canadians." *Health* 34, no. 5 (October 1966): 12-13, 26-28.

Brennan, Michael J., Taft, Philip, and Schupack, Mark B. *The Economics of Age.* New York: Norton, 1967.

Brownstone, Meyer. "Economic Needs and Employment of the Aged." Background paper prepared for the Canadian Conference on Aging, 1966. Ottawa: Canadian Welfare Council, 1966.

Bryden, Kenneth. *Old Age Pensions and Policy-Making in Canada.* Montreal: McGill-Queen's University Press, 1974.

Canada. Department of National Health and Welfare. Research and Statistics Directorate. *New Dimensions in Aging.* Ottawa: Queen's Printer, 1968.

Canada. Department of National Health and Welfare. Research and Statistics Division. *Services for the Aged in Canada.* Ottawa: Department of National Health and Welfare, 1957.

Canada. Dominion Bureau of Statistics. *Selected Statistics on the Older Population of Canada.* Ottawa: Queen's Printer, 1964.

Canada. Ministère de la Santé nationale et du Bien-être social. Division de la recherche et des statistiques. *Mesures législatives applicables au logement des personnes âgées au Canada.* Série générale, mémoire n° 16. Ottawa: Ministère de la Santé nationale et du Bien-être social, 1961.

Canada. Parlement. Chambre des communes. Comité permanent de la santé, du bien-être social et des affaires sociales. *Procès-verbaux et témoignages concernant: Bill C-22, loi modifiant le régime de pensions du Canada.* N° 3, 29 octobre 1974. Ottawa: Information Canada, 1974a.

Canada. Parlement. Chambre des communes. Comité permanent de la santé, du bien-être social et des affaires sociales. *Procès-verbaux et témoignages concernant: Bill C-62, loi sur la sécurité de la vieillesse.* N° 26, 17 juin 1975. Ottawa: Information Canada, 1975a.

Canada. Parliament. Senate. Special Committee on Aging. *Minutes of Proceedings.* No. 1, 17 October 1963. Ottawa: Queen's Printer, 1963.

Canada. Parliament. Senate. Special Committee on Aging. *Minutes of Proceedings.* No. 2, 24 October 1963. Ottawa: Queen's Printer, 1963.

Canada. Parliament. Senate. Special Committee on Aging. *Minutes of Proceedings.* No. 14, 2 July 1964. Ottawa: Queen's Printer, 1964.

Canada. Parliament. Senate. Special Committee on Aging. *Minutes of Proceedings.* No. 15, 9 July 1964. Ottawa: Queen's Printer, 1964.

Canada. Parliament. Senate. Special Committee on Aging. *Final Report.* Ottawa: Queen's Printer, 1966.

Canadian Welfare Council. *At Home After 65: Housing and Related Services for the Aging.* Ottawa: Canadian Welfare Council, 1964a.

Canadian Welfare Council. *Proceedings of the Canadian Conference on Aging.* Toronto, 20–24 January 1966. Ottawa: Canadian Welfare Council, 1966a.

Canadian Welfare Council. *Study on Housing for the Aged: Final Report.* Ottawa: Canadian Welfare Council, 1964b.

Canadian Welfare Council. Committee on Aging. *The Aging in Canada, 1966.* Ottawa: Canadian Welfare Council, 1966b.

Chaddock, R. E. "Age and Sex in Population Analysis." *Annals of the American Academy of Political and Social Science* 188 (November 1936): 185–93.

Clark, J. A., and Collishaw, N. E. "Canada's Older Population." Working paper. Ottawa: Department of National Health and Welfare, 1975.

Crawford, Lawrence, and St. Michael Guinan, Sister. "Current Research on Aging." Paper prepared for the Ontario Long Term Study on Aging. Toronto: Ministry of Community and Social Services, 1973.

Crawford, Marion P. "Retirement and Disengagement." *Human Relations* 24, no. 3 (June 1971): 255-78.

Dion, Léon. "Political Impact of the Changing Age Structure." Summary of a paper presented at the Science Council Committee on Population and Technology, Working Party on the Implications of a Changing Age Structure, Ottawa, January 1975.

Douglass, Elizabeth, Cleveland, William P., and Maddox, George L. "Political Attitudes, Age, and Aging: A Cohort Analysis of Archival Data." *Journal of Gerontology* 29, no. 6 (November 1974): 666-75.

Durand, J. D. "The Trend Toward the Older Population." *Annals of the American Academy of Political and Social Science* 237 (January 1945): 142-51.

Environics Research Group. *The Elderly and their Environment: A Pilot Enquiry into Senior Citizens' Housing Satisfaction.* Ottawa: Central Mortgage and Housing Corporation, 1972a.

Environics Research Group. *The Seventh Age: A Bibliography of Canadian Sources in Gerontology and Geriatrics, 1964-1972.* Ottawa: Central Mortgage and Housing Corporation, 1972b.

Ferguson, Elizabeth. *Income, Resources and Needs of Older People.* New York: National Council on the Aging, 1964.

Field, Minna. *Depth and Extent of the Geriatric Problem.* Springfield, Ill.: Thomas, 1970.

Garrett, Lorna, and Hill, Mary. *A Study of Community Care for Seniors.* Vancouver: Social Planning and Review Council of B.C., 1972.

Havens, B., and Thompson, E. *Design for Matching Needs of and Resources for the Elderly in Manitoba.* Winnipeg: Department of Health and Social Development, Planning and Program Development, Division of Research, 1972.

Kleemeier, Robert Watson, ed. *Aging and Leisure; A Research Perspective into the Meaningful Use of Time.* New York: Oxford University Press, 1961.

Krislov, Joseph. "Four Issues in Income Maintenance for the Aged During the 1970's." *Social Service Review* 42, no. 3 (September 1968): 335-43.

Lalonde, Marc. "Age is Opportunity." Notes for an address by the Minister of National Health and Welfare on the role of the senior citizens in the Canadian community: a positive force, Winnipeg, 29 May 1974.

Lalonde, Marc. Notes for an address by the Minister of National Health and Welfare to the National Pensioners and Senior Citizens Federation, Regina, 22 September 1975.

Lawton, M. Powell, and Cohen, Jacob. "The Generality of Housing Impact on the Well-Being of Older People." *Journal of Gerontology* 29, no. 2 (March 1974): 194–204.

Loether, Herman. *Problem of Aging: Sociological and Psychological Perspectives.* Belmont: Dickinson Publishing, 1967.

Lyons, Walter. "Services to the Aged Beyond the Institutional Setting — 'What is Our Responsibility?'" *Canadian Welfare* 42, no. 1 (January/ February 1966): 2–7.

Manitoba. Department of Health and Welfare. Planning and Program Development. Division of Research. *Field Survey of Needs of the Elderly and Resources to Meet Needs in Manitoba.* Winnipeg: Queen's Printer, 1972.

Markus, Nathan. "Home Care for the Aged." *Canadian Welfare* 50, no. 1 (January/February 1974): 16–19, 30–31.

Neugarten, Bernice L., ed. "Aging in the Year 2000: A Look at the Future." *Gerontologist* 15, no. 1 (February 1975).

Ontario. Legislative Assembly. Select Committee on Aging. *Final Recommendations.* Toronto: Queen's Printer, 1967.

Ontario Society on Aging. *Aging is Everyone's Concern.* Proceedings of the First Ontario Conference on Aging held at the University of Toronto, 31 May to 30 June 1957. Toronto: Ontario Society on Aging, 1958.

Ontario Society on Aging. *Workshop on Aging,* held in Toronto, 26 March 1960. Toronto: Ontario Society on Aging, 1960.

Ontario Welfare Council. *Economic Needs and Resources of Older People in Ontario.* Report of the Committee on Public Welfare Policy. Toronto: Ontario Welfare Council, 1959.

Orback, Harold, and Tibbitts, Clark, eds. *Aging and the Economy.* Ann Arbor, Mich.: University of Michigan Press, 1963.

Ostry, Sylvia, and Podoluk, Jenny. *The Economic Status of the Aging.* Ottawa: Dominion Bureau of Statistics, 1966.

Riley, Matilda W., Johnson, Marilyn E., and Foner, Anne. *Aging and Society.* Vol. 3: *A Sociology of Age Stratification.* New York: Russell Sage Foundation, 1972.

Rombout, Mary K. "Les hôpitaux et les personnes âgées: tendances actuelles et futures." Notes de recherche. Ottawa: Ministère de la Santé nationale et du Bien-être social, 1975.

Rose, Arnold M. "Aging and Social Change: Implications and Challenges." In *Social Change and Aging in the 20th Century,* edited by Daniel E. Alleger. Gainesville, Fla.: University of Florida Press, 1964.

Saskatchewan. Aged and Long Term Illness Survey Committee. *Report and Recommendations.* Regina: Queen's Printer, 1963.

Saskatchewan. Senior Citizen's Commission. *A Report by the Senior Citizen's Commission.* Regina: Department of Social Services, 1974.

Sauvy, A. "Social and Economic Consequences of Ageing of Western European Populations." *Population Studies* 2, no. 1 (June 1948): 115–24.

Social Planning and Review Council of B.C. *A Study of Community Care for Seniors.* Vancouver: Social Planning and Review Council of B.C., 1972.

Tobin, Sheldon S. "Social and Health Services for the Future Aged." *Gerontologist* 15 (February 1975): 32–37.

United Nations. *The Aging of Populations and Its Economic and Social Implications.* Population Studies, no. 26. New York: United Nations, 1956.

United Nations. *Some Quantitative Aspects of the Aging of Western Populations.* Population Bulletin, no. 1. New York: United Nations, 1951.

U.S. Congress. Joint Economic Committee. *Old Age Income Assurance: A Compendium of Papers on Problems and Policy Issues in the Public and Private Pension System.* Submitted to the Subcommittee on Fiscal Policy. Committee Print. Washington, D.C.: Government Printing Office, 1967–1968.

U.S. Congress. Senate. *Economics of Aging, Toward a Full Share in Abundance.* Report of the Special Committee on Aging. S. Rept. 1548, 91st Cong., 1st and 2d sess., 1969-1970.

U.S. Congress. Senate. *Older Americans and Transportation: A Crisis in Mobility.* Report of the Special Committee on Aging. S. Rept. 1520, 91st Cong., 2d sess., 1970.

U.S. Congress. Senate. Special Committee on Aging. *Long-Range Program and Research Needs in Aging and Related Fields. Hearings.* 90th Cong., 1st sess., 1968.

U.S. Department of Health, Education and Welfare. *Aging, 1951-.* Washington, D.C.: Government Printing Office, 1974.

U.S. Department of Health, Education and Welfare. *The Nation and Its Older People.* Report of the White House Conference on Aging, 9–12 January 1961. Washington, D.C.: Government Printing Office, 1961.

U.S. Department of Health, Education and Welfare. Social Security Administration. *The Economic Status of the Retired Aged in 1980: Simulation Projections,* by James H. Schulz. Washington, D.C.: Government Printing Office, 1968.

U.S. President's Task Force on Aging. *Toward a Brighter Future for the Elderly.* Washington, D.C.: Government Printing Office, 1970.

U.S. White House Conference on Aging (1971). *Recommended for Action: Retirement Roles and Activities.* Washington, D.C.: Government Printing Office, 1972.

Wilson, Lola. "Leisure." Background paper prepared for the Canadian Conference on Aging, 1966. Ottawa: Canadian Welfare Council, 1966.

Wilson, Lola. Rapport de la session de formation à l'intention des directeurs de centres pour personnes âgées, Winnipeg, 29 février 1972. Ottawa: Ministère de la Santé nationale et du Bien-être social, 1972.

Winnipeg Foundation. *First Manitoba Conference on Aging: Report of Proceedings,* 29–31 May 1958. Winnipeg: Winnipeg Foundation, 1958.

Zay, N. "Living Arrangements for the Aged." Background paper prepared for the Canadian Conference on Aging, 1966. Ottawa: Canadian Welfare Council, 1966.

Regional Development

Archour, Dominique. "Projections démo-économiques communauté régionale de l'Outaouais." Montréal: Université de Montréal, Centre de recherches et d'innovation urbaines, 1974.

Canada. Statistics Canada. *1971 Census of Canada.* Vol. 1 (Part 1): *Population — Census Subdivisions (Historical).* Cat. No. 92-702. Ottawa: Information Canada, 1973.

Canadian Council on Rural Development. *Commitment to Rural Canada.* Fifth Report and Review. Ottawa: Information Canada, 1973.

Canadian Council on Rural Development. *Rural Canada, 1970: Prospects and Problems.* Ottawa: Information Canada, 1970.

Chisholm, Michael. "Regional Policies for the 1970's." *Geographical Journal,* June 1974, pp. 215-44.

Dyck, Harold, and Emery, George J. *Social Futures: Alberta 1970–2005.* Edmonton: Human Resources Research Council of Alberta, 1970.

Economic Council of Canada. Working Group on Regional and Urban Policy Analysis. "A Research Agenda for Regional and Urban Policy Studies." Ottawa: Economic Council of Canada, 1974.

George, M.V., and Gnanasekaran, K.S. *Population and Labour Force Projections for Alberta, 1970-1985.* Edmonton: Human Resources Research Council of Alberta, 1972.

Henripin, Jacques, et Légaré, Jacques. *Évolution démographique du Québec et de ses régions, 1966-1986.* Québec: Presses de l'Université Laval, 1969.

Maki, W.R., Framingham, C.F., and Sandell, D.J. *Population Projections for Manitoba by Region and Town Size — Some Alternatives, 1971-1990.* Research Bulletin, no. 73-2. Winnipeg: University of Manitoba, Faculty of Agriculture, Department of Agricultural Economics and Farm Management, 1973.

Manitoba. Commission on Targets for Economic Development. *Manitoba to 1980; Report.* Winnipeg: Queen's Printer, 1969.

Nicholls, William M. *Views on Rural Development in Canada.* Canadian Council on Rural Development, Special Study, no. 1. Ottawa: Queen's Printer, 1968.

Ontario. Department of Economics and Development. Economics Branch. *Population and Labour Force Projections for the Economic Regions of Ontario, 1961-1986.* Toronto: Department of Economics and Development, 1964.

Ontario. Department of Treasury and Economics. *Ontario Labour Force Projections, 1968-1991.* Toronto: Department of Treasury and Economics, 1968.

Ontario Economic Council. *Human Resource Development in the Province of Ontario.* Toronto: Ontario Economic Council, 1965.

Parks, A.C. *Recent Population Trends: Atlantic Provinces.* Halifax: Atlantic Provinces Economic Council, 1968.

Québec: Bureau de la statistique. Section démographique. *Perspectives démographiques, 1961-2001.* Québec: Bureau de la statistique, 1968.

Québec. Bureau de la statistique. Service de la démographie et du recensement. *Perspective d'évolution de la population de Québec et des régions administratives scolaires, 1971-1986.* Québec: Bureau de la statistique, 1974.

Ward, E. Neville, and Cranmer, Valerie. "Canada Has Land 'Crises' from Sea to Sea." *Canadian Geographical Journal* 89, no. 6 (December 1974): 34-41.

Social Welfare and Social Services

Adams, Ian, Cameron, William, Hill, Brian, and Penz, Peter. *The Real Poverty Report.* Edmonton: Hurtig, 1971.

Canada. Department of National Health and Welfare. *Social Security in Canada*. Ottawa: Information Canada, 1974b.

Canada. Department of National Health and Welfare. *Working Paper on Social Security in Canada*. Ottawa: Department of National Health and Welfare, 1973c.

Canada. Department of National Health and Welfare. Policy Research Planning and Evaluation Branch. *Social Security and Public Welfare Services in Canada, 1972*. Ottawa: Department of National Health and Welfare, 1972.

Canada. Federal-Provincial Meeting of Welfare Ministers, Edmonton, 19–20 February 1974. *Communiqué*.

Canada. Federal-Provincial Meeting of Welfare Ministers, Ottawa, 19–20 November 1974. *Communiqué*.

Canada. Federal-Provincial Meeting of Welfare Ministers, Ottawa, 18–19 February 1975. *Communiqué*.

Canada. Federal-Provincial Meeting of Welfare Ministers, Ottawa, 30 April, 1 May 1975. *Communiqué*.

Canada. Parliament. Senate. Special Committee on Poverty. *Poverty in Canada*. Ottawa: Information Canada, 1971.

Canadian Council on Social Development. *Social Security for Canada 1973*. Ottawa: Canadian Council on Social Development, 1973.

Cummings, Raymond J., et al., eds. *Public Welfare and Employment — Related Services: A Preliminary Annotated Bibliography*. Minneapolis: Institute for Interdisciplinary Studies, 1970.

Hepworth, H. Philip. *Personal Social Services in Canada: A Review*. Vol. 9: *The Personal Social Services in Context*. Ottawa: Canadian Council on Social Development, 1975b.

Urban and Metropolitan Affairs

Alonso, William. "What are New Towns For?" *Urban Studies* 7, no. 1 (1970): 37–55.

Armstrong, Alan H. "Emerging Urban Land Policy in Canada." Notes for a Colloquy on National Land Policies held by the American Society of Planning Officials, New York, 8 April 1970. Ottawa: Canadian Council on Urban and Regional Research, 1970.

Atlantic Development Board. *Urban Centres in the Atlantic Provinces*. Background Study, no. 7. Ottawa: Queen's Printer, 1969.

Basford, Ron. "Approche tripartite à la gestion de la croissance." Discours du Ministre d'État aux Affaires urbaines à la deuxième conférence tripartite, Edmonton, 22 octobre 1973a.

Basford, Ron. Discours du Ministre d'État aux Affaires urbaines à la première conférence tripartite, Toronto, 21 novembre 1972.

Basford, Ron. "Le transport." Discours du Ministre d'État aux Affaires urbaines à la deuxième conférence tripartite, Edmonton, 22 octobre 1973d.

Bourne, Larry S., MacKinnon, R. D., Siegel, J., and Simmons, J.W. *Urban Futures for Central Canada: Perspectives on Forecasting Urban Growth and Form.* Toronto: University of Toronto Press, 1974.

Cadbury, George. "A Population Policy? The Present Situation." In *A Population Policy for Canada?* Proceedings of 2 seminars: "The Need for a Canadian Population Policy," held at the Ontario Institute for Studies in Education, Toronto, 20–21 November 1972, and "The Impact of People on the Environment," held at United Church House, Toronto, 10–11 May 1973. Toronto: Family Planning Federation of Canada, 1973.

Canada. Federal Task Force on Housing and Urban Development. "Impressions." In *Critical Issues in Canadian Society,* edited by C. Boydell et al. Toronto: Holt, Rinehart and Winston, 1971.

Canada. Ministère d'État aux Affaires urbaines. "Consultation tripartite historique." Communiqué: dossier consultation tripartite. Ottawa: 20 novembre 1972a.

Canada. Ministère d'État aux Affaires urbaines. "La consultation tripartite sur une base régionale est amorcée." Communiqué: dossier consultation tripartite. Ottawa: 20 novembre 1972b.

Canada. Ministère d'État aux Affaires urbaines. "L'impact fédéral sur l'urbanisation." Communiqué: dossier consultation tripartite. Ottawa: 20 novembre 1972c.

Canada. Ministère d'État aux Affaires urbaines. "Ottawa se dit prêt à participer à une consultation tripartite permanente." Communiqué: dossier consultation tripartite. Ottawa: 20 novembre 1972d.

Canada. Ministère d'État aux Affaires urbaines. "Les vues du gouvernement fédéral sur la conférence tripartite." Communiqué: dossier consultation tripartite. Ottawa: 20 novembre 1972e.

Canada. Ministère d'État aux Affaires urbaines. *Le D.E.C.A.U.: le fédéral face à l'urbanisation.* Ottawa: Ministère d'État aux Affaires urbaines, 1974a.

Canada. Ministère d'État aux Affaires urbaines. *Rapport annuel pour l'exercice financier terminé le 31 mars 1973.* Ottawa: Ministère d'État aux Affaires urbaines, 1974b.

Canada. Ministry of State for Urban Affairs. *Annual Report 1973–74.* Ottawa: Information Canada, 1975a.

Canada. Ministry of State for Urban Affairs. Demographic Research Group. Policy and Research Wing. "Interim Population Projections of 22 Census Metropolitan Areas, 1971-2001." Discussion paper B75.10. Ottawa: Ministry of State for Urban Affairs, 1975b.

Canada. Parlement. Chambre des communes. Comité permanent de la santé, du bien-être social et des affaires sociales. *Procès-verbaux et témoignages concernant: Budget principal 1974-1975, Département d'État chargé des Affaires urbaines.* N° 1, 15 octobre 1974. Ottawa: Information Canada, 1974b.

Canada. Statistics Canada. *1971 Census of Canada.* Vol. I (Part 1): *Population — Urban and Rural Distributions.* Cat. No. 92-709. Ottawa: Information Canada, 1973.

Canada. Statistics Canada. *1971 Census of Canada.* Vol. 2 (Part 3): *Housing — Dwellings by Tenure and Structural Type.* Cat. No. 93-727. Ottawa: Information Canada, 1973.

Canada. Task Force on Housing and Urban Development. *Report.* Ottawa: Queen's Printer, 1969.

Canadian Federation of Mayors and Municipalities. *Forecast of Urban Growth Problems and Requirements, 1956-1980.* Montreal: The Federation, 1956.

Chevalier, Michel. "Urban Growth and Development: The Shape of Things to Come." *Architecture Canada* 44 (July 1967): 44-46.

Chevalier, Michel, et Chouckroun, Jean-Marc. "Un modèle de changement urbain au Canada." *Sociologie et Sociétés* 4, n° 1 (mai 1972): 83-99.

Conférence tripartite nationale, 1ʳᵉ, Toronto. *Exposés de la position fédérale.* Ottawa: Ministère d'État aux Affaires urbaines, 1972.

Conférence tripartite nationale, 2ᵉ, Edmonton. *Exposés de la position fédérale.* Ottawa: Ministère d'Etat aux Affaires urbaines, 1973.

Danson, Barney. Notes for an address by the Minister of State for Urban Affairs to the Canadian Institute of Public Affairs, Toronto, 25 January 1975a.

Danson, Barney. Notes for an address by the Minister of State for Urban Affairs to the 38th Annual Conference of the Canadian Federation of Mayors and Municipalities, London, Ontario, 2 June 1975b.

Danson, Barney. "An Urban Strategy for Canada." Notes for an address by the Minister of State for Urban Affairs to the Conference Board in Canada, Winnipeg, 2 April 1975c.

Danson, Barney. "The Way to Habitat." Notes for an address by the Minister of State for Urban Affairs to the National Joint Conference of the American Society of Planning Officials and the Community Planning Association of Canada, Vancouver, 15 April 1975d.

Edmonton, Alta. City Planning Department. *Metropolitan Edmonton Population Projections, 1971–2001.* Edmonton: City of Edmonton Planning Department, 1971.

Gertler, L. O. "Urban Shadow, Urban Theory and Regional Planning." In *Regional Planning in Canada: A Planners Testament,* pp. 34–47. Montreal: Harvest House, 1972.

Goracz, A., Lithwick, I., and Stone, L. O. *The Urban Future.* Research Monograph, no. 5. Ottawa: Central Mortgage and Housing Corporation, 1971.

Haar, Charles M. *The President's Task Force on Suburban Problems.* Cambridge, Mass.: Ballinger Publishing Co., 1974.

Hellyer, Paul. "Cities of the Future: Heaven or Hell?" *Queen's Quarterly* 78, no. 2 (Summer 1971): 168–74.

Judd, Dennis L. Review of *Urban Politics and Public Policy,* 2nd ed., by Robert L. Lineberry and Ira Sharkansky. *Urban Affairs Quarterly,* September 1974, pp. 95–101.

Klunder, Hans. Review of *Analysis of Municipal Development and Financial Evaluation of Urban Growth: A Study Related to Small Town Planning,* by Herbert Grabe. *Journal of American Institute of Planners,* March 1975, pp. 124–25.

Krueger, Ralph R., and Bryfogle, R. Charles, eds. *Urban Problems: A Canadian Reader.* Toronto: Holt, Rinehart and Winston, 1971.

Lithwick, N. H. *Urban Canada: Problems and Prospects.* Ottawa: Central Mortgage and Housing Corporation, 1970.

Lithwick, N. H., and Paquet, G. *Urban Studies: A Canadian Perspective.* Toronto: Methuen, 1968.

Metropolitan Corporation of Greater Winnipeg, Manitoba. Planning Division. *The City of Winnipeg Population Projections, 1966–1996.* Winnipeg: Metropolitan Corporation of Greater Winnipeg, Planning Divison, 1972.

Metropolitan Toronto, Ontario. Planning Board. Research Division. *Labour Force and Employment Projections 1966–2001, Metropolitan Toronto Planning Area, Ontario and Canada.* Metropolitan Plan Review Report, no. 3. Toronto: Metropolitan Toronto Planning Board, 1969.

Metropolitan Toronto, Ontario. Planning Board. Research Division. *Population Projections 1966–2001, Metropolitan Toronto Planning Area, Ontario and Canada.* Metropolitan Plan Review Report, no. 2. Toronto: Metropolitan Toronto Planning Board, 1968.

Miles, Simon, Cohen, Sharon, and de Koenig, Geert. *Developing a Canadian Urban Policy: Some Problems and Proposals.* Metropolitan Studies Series, 3. Toronto: Intermet, 1973.

101

Mills, Edwin S. "Welfare Aspects of National Policy Towards City Sizes." *Urban Studies* 9, no. 1 (1972): 117–24.

Municipality of Metropolitan Toronto. *Choices for the Future. Summary Report: Metropolitan Toronto Transportation Plan Review.* Toronto: Ministry of Transportation and Communications, 1975.

Québec. Ministère des Affaires municipales. *L'urbanisation au Québec: Rapport du groupe de travail sur l'urbanisation* (Rapport Castonguay). Québec: Éditeur officiel du Québec, 1976.

Reynolds, D.J. *Urban Transport Problem.* Research Monograph, no. 3. Ottawa: Central Mortgage and Housing Corporation, 1971.

Richardson, Boyce. *The Future of Canadian Cities.* Toronto: New Press, 1972.

Saicans, André. *Prévisions démographiques des régions administratives et des principales agglomérations urbaines, 1976-2001.* Annexe III. Québec: Office de planification et de développement du Québec, 1973.

Schmid, Allan A. *Converting Land from Rural to Urban Uses.* Washington, D.C.: Resources for the Future, 1968.

Science Council of Canada. *Cities for Tomorrow: Some Applications of Science and Technology to Urban Development.* Science Council of Canada, Report, no. 14. Ottawa: Information Canada, 1971b.

Stone, Leroy O. *Urban Development in Canada.* 1961 Census Monograph. Ottawa: Queen's Printer, 1967.

Thompson, W.R. "The Rational System of Cities as an Object of Public Policy." *Urban Studies* 9, no. 1 (1972): 99–116.

Thompson, Wilbur R. "Urban Research and Policy Planning." In *Urban Research and Policy Planning,* edited by C.L.F. Schmore and H. Fagin, pp. 142–43. Beverly Hills: Sage Publications, 1967.

Wingo, Lowdon. "Issues in a National Urban Development Strategy for the United States." *Urban Studies* 9, no. 1 (1972): 3–27.

Miscellaneous

Alberta. Lieutenant Governor. *Speeches from the Throne.* Edmonton: Queen's Printer, 1974-1975.

Bakony, L.I. *Household Demand for Telecommunications Services — A Projection to 1980.* Telecommission Study 2 (b) (ii). Ottawa: Information Canada, 1971.

Basford, Ron. "Les finances publiques." Discours du Ministre d'État aux Affaires urbaines à la deuxième conférence tripartite, Edmonton, 22 octobre 1973a.

Bogue, Donald. *Principles of Demography.* New York: Wiley, 1969.

Boydell, Craig L., Grindstaff, Carl F., and Whitehead, Paul C., eds. *Critical Issues in Canadian Society.* Toronto: Holt, Rinehart and Winston, 1971.

British Columbia. Lieutenant Governor. *Speeches from the Throne.* Victoria: Queen's Printer, 1974–1975.

Canada. Commission royale d'enquête sur la situation de la femme au Canada. *Rapport.* Ottawa: Information Canada, 1970.

Canada. Statistics Canada. *1971 Census of Canada.* Vol. 2 (Part 1): *Households — Households by Size.* Cat. No. 93–702. Ottawa: Information Canada, 1973.

Canada. Statistics Canada. *1971 Census of Canada.* Vol. 2 (Part 2): *Families — Families by Size and Type.* Cat. No. 93–714. Ottawa: Information Canada, 1973.

Chrétien, Jean. Discours du Président du Conseil du Trésor devant l'Association des anciens élèves de l'Université Laval, 3 octobre 1975. *Le Devoir,* 11 octobre 1975, p. 5.

Clark, Richard S. "Notes on Transportation Trends and Implications." Paper prepared for the Science Council Committee on Population and Technology, Ottawa, 1975.

Culley, Eric. "Forecasting Intercity Travel." Paper presented to the Sixth Annual Meeting of the Canadian Transportation Research Forum, Winnipeg, 1970. Ottawa: Canadian Transport Commission, Research Division, 1970.

Dobson, Wendy. "National Population Objectives Are Slowly Taking Shape, Now We Need Policies." *Science Forum* 8 (December 1975): 24-27.

Economic Council of Canada. *Fourth Annual Review: The Canadian Economy from the 1960's to the 1970's.* Ottawa: Queen's Printer, 1967.

Economic Council of Canada. *Eighth Annual Review: Design for Decision-Making — An Application to Human Resources Policies.* Ottawa: Information Canada, 1971.

Furniss, Norman. "The Practical Significance of Decentralization." *Journal of Politics* 36, no. 4 (November 1974): 958-82.

Goracz, A. "Housing Requirements to 1980." Technical Paper, No. 3. Ottawa: Central Mortgage and Housing Corporation, 1969.

Kirkland, John S. *Demographic Aspects of Housing Demand to 1986.* Ottawa: Central Mortgage and Housing Corporation, 1971.

Lachapelle, Réjean. "Préoccupations politiques et tendances démographiques." Paper prepared for the Institute for Research on Public Policy. Montreal: 1975b.

Lockhead, Douglas. *Bibliography of Canadian Bibliographies.* Toronto: University of Toronto Press, 1972.

Manitoba. Lieutenant Governor. *Speeches from the Throne.* Winnipeg: Queen's Printer, 1974–1975.

Marsden, Lorna R. *Population Probe.* Toronto: Copp Clark, 1972.

New Brunswick. Lieutenant Governor. *Speeches from the Throne.* Fredericton: Queen's Printer, 1974-1975.

Newfoundland. Lieutenant Governor. *Speeches from the Throne.* St. John's: Queen's Printer, 1974–1975.

Nova Scotia. Lieutenant Governor. *Speeches from the Throne.* Halifax: Queen's Printer, 1974-1975.

Ontario. Lieutenant Governor. *Speeches from the Throne.* Toronto: Queen's Printer, 1974–1975.

Prince Edward Island. Lieutenant Governor. *Speeches from the Throne.* Charlottetown: Queen's Printer, 1974–1975.

Québec. Lieutenant-gouverneur. *Messages d'ouverture.* Québec: Éditeur officiel du Québec, 1974-1975.

Saskatchewan. Lieutenant Governor. *Speeches from the Throne.* Regina: Queen's Printer, 1974–1975.

Science Council of Canada. *Annual Report 1970–1971.* Ottawa: Information Canada, 1971.

Shea, Albert A. *Canada 1980.* Toronto: McClelland & Stewart, 1960.

Systems Research Group. *Canada: Family, Households and Housing Projections to the Year 2000.* Toronto: Systems Research Group, 1970a.

Systems Research Group. *Canada: Transportation Projections to the Year 2000.* Toronto: Systems Research Group, 1970c.

United Nations. *The Determinants and Consequences of Population Trends.* Population Studies, no. 50. New York: United Nations, 1973.

U.S. Department of Health, Education and Welfare. *Toward a Social Report.* Washington, D.C.: Government Printing Office, 1969.

Wall Street Journal. *Here Comes Tomorrow! Living and Working in the Year 2000.* By the staff of the Wall Street Journal. Princeton, N.J.: Dow Jones Books, 1967.

INDEX